Supporting Behavioural, Emotional and Social Difficulties in School

Teachers need to be equipped not only to teach, but also to help build mental security and wellbeing into the lives of young people and children. *Supporting Behavioural, Emotional and Social Difficulties in School* provides practical, relevant and proven strategies and constructive advice in order to guide teachers in this endeavour, helping them to both understand and overcome the difficulties and generational changes faced by young people and children.

Containing information on topics such as classroom strategies for common issues; first impressions; and how to deal with adults, leadership and tasks such as school trips, this volume presents tried and tested strategies and shares the author's knowledge when it comes to working in all types of schools, including primary, secondary, and pupil referral units. Not only exploring the strategies, this book also examines the reasons why a situation has arisen, and, for each piece of advice, offers an explanation for why it will work and how it affects our sense of coherence. The book also includes a short introduction to brain development at various ages, exploring the implications for children as they grow and mature, as well as examining how teachers can work with and help children through these developmental stages, assisting teachers in understanding the factors to be aware of when helping students and children develop mental security.

Consolidating an understanding of mental and emotional health issues within children and young people, knowledge about cognitive brain development, and advice on what teachers can do in their classroom to make a difference, this book is essential reading for all teachers.

Victor Allen is a freelance consultant in the educational and business sector, advising on teaching ways of improving all aspects of emotional, social and mental wellbeing for children, staff and leaders.

T0347523

Supporting Behavioural, Emotional and Social Difficulties in School

A Strategy a Day for a Calm Learning Environment

Victor Allen

Routledge
Taylor & Francis Group

LONDON AND NEW YORK

First published 2020
by Routledge
2 Park Square, Milton Park, Abingdon, Oxon OX14 4RN

and by Routledge
52 Vanderbilt Avenue, New York, NY 10017

Routledge is an imprint of the Taylor & Francis Group, an informa business

British Library Cataloguing-in-Publication Data
A catalogue record for this book is available from the British Library

Library of Congress Cataloging-in-Publication Data
A catalog record has been requested for this book

ISBN: 978-0-367-49462-9 (hbk)
ISBN: 978-0-367-34183-1 (pbk)
ISBN: 978-0-429-32434-5 (ebk)

Typeset in Sabon
by Swales & Willis, Exeter, Devon, UK

Contents

Contents

Dedication and acknowledgements

I dedicate this book to all the teachers and support staff who embark on their careers in order to make a difference in the lives of the young people they teach and nurture. Over the years I have met some amazing, influential unsung heroes, daily going that extra mile to improve the mental wellbeing and social and emotional development of those within their schools. Manu, Cath, Michelle, Jonny, Paul, Esther, Sarah, Matthew, Sonia, Marie, Ian – these are just a few of the people who instantly spring to mind whom I know have impacted, for the better, the lives within their influence. Also, to those I have met and have said 'I am impressed', this book is for you. Thank you for all you constantly do for others.

I also want to dedicate it to my wife Sonia for her constant support and encouragement to me. Her patience, care and help is a constant blessing, along with her wisdom on all issues relating to SEND. I would like also to thank her for writing the SEND section in this book.

To our grandchildren, Lyra and Leo, thank you for providing us both with such wonderful fun memories and close hand observations of all stages of growing up.

To my daughters, Laura and Esther, who, in their own special, insightful and caring way, are making a difference in the young people they support and look after: I am immensely proud of you and your work.

And finally, to Helen Fairlie, who once again through her tireless and excellent work helps bring my thoughts and ideas onto paper. I am so glad she is here to help.

Introduction

Why is this book needed now?

A teacher's job has changed beyond recognition over the past 30 years. The expected professionalism and expertise needed to do well within this demanding, yet immensely rewarding area of work is constantly changing. Throughout their career teachers are having to keep an eye on the latest changes and developments in knowledge, new technology and equipment to help them deliver their lessons, as well as being scrutinised often by an inspection system which is itself frequently shifting. On top of this they are having to deal with increased pressure in the classroom from children and teenagers who are showing signs of increased mental health issues, a rise in family conflict and other issues affecting the mental wellbeing of students in a fluctuating and changing social environment.

Quite often teachers are also now dealing with and assimilating into the classroom students and children who, because of changes within society and the wider world, come from different cultural, social and economic backgrounds.

Those born after 1996 are known as Generation Z; they are the first fully digital generation. The age for acquiring their first smart phone continues to drop and in 2018 it was reported that 95% of 13–22-year-olds had a smartphone (The Center for Generational Kinetics, 2018). The influence of these devices seeps into their sleeping hours, impacting on their ability to function at school. Sixty-five percent of young people are using their smart phones after midnight a few times a week! What are Generation Z doing on their phones? They're engaging with social media. For them, social media is the best way to stay in contact with the world and their friends.

To learn all the aspects of social and emotional intelligence they will need your help and support. All of these challenges form the backdrop against which teachers must get on and do the day-to-day job of teaching.

This book aims to help support you as a teacher and provide you with practical, relevant and proven strategies and constructive advice to help overcome and understand the difficulties and generational changes faced by young people. I hope it will help you not only to remain in the profession but survive and experience all the emotional and social benefits which come from assisting and teaching young people and children in the twenty-first century. It will also provide insights as to the foundation which I believe is needed to help build up socially and emotionally competent young people.

As a teacher you need to be equipped to teach your chosen subjects but also to help lay a foundation which builds mental security and wellbeing into the lives of our young people and children to enable them to thrive in this ever changing and challenging world.

Teachers are often tempted to look for quick fixes to deal with issues and emotional problems that children and young people have, when these issues may have taken weeks, months or sometimes years in the making. I hope to help you realise that each person you are working with and teaching will have their own view of the world. Perhaps they have found ways that to them help them manage life as best they can, but their strategies may in fact be detrimental to their own future, e.g. shouting at people in authority when they become frustrated. Some of these strategies you may be able to use, and they will meet an immediate need and be successful, but others will need to be looked at as a longer project. To help children and young people to change will often take time, but each step that you take in building a relationship and trying to understand them adds to the improvement of their lives. No act of kindness is a waste of time. My aim is always to help children and students to learn to control themselves and learn to manage their own emotions. As we all know this takes time, and we don't always get it right, but it is far better that the time is taken and they learn these important life skills, than they have teachers and other adults 'controlling' them.

What's in this book?

Whether you are new to the profession or just looking for strategies, within these pages you will find something that will help you.

Each piece of advice includes the reasons why it will work, either socially, or emotionally, how it affects our sense of coherence as outlined in the 3Ms (see Chapter 1), as well as offering some practical help as to what to try. I have also tried to cover, along with issues you will find in your classroom, strategies for all other aspects of your teaching career as you widen your experiences. Advancement and promotion can be rapid, and sometimes the training needed to fully meet the new demands is slow to catch up, so the strategies and advice contained within the book will help you prepare and make a good start. The best learning you will have for all you will experience will be within your own classroom. The many issues you face on a day-to-day basis with children and young people are very similar to issues you will encounter when dealing with adults. We all have the same emotional and social brain and most of us react in similar ways either because of the hard-wired nature of our brain or the similar social and emotional experiences we have encountered. Get used to learning and not being surprised at what folks do. You aim is to understand, first and foremost. Assume nothing, because as the adage goes, to assume makes an **ass** out of **u** and **me**.

The book is in three parts. Part 1 will provide you with a short introduction to brain development at various ages, exploring the implications for children as they grow and mature, as well as looking at how teachers can work with and help children through these stages. It will also provide you with an introduction to the factors to be aware of when helping students and children to develop mental security. Part 2 covers general strategies for working in primary and secondary schools, and Part 3 contains detailed specific strategies for how you might best manage the common scenarios you will come across in your daily work.

Feedback is important, so I would love to know what you have tried and how successful it was, as well as letting me know if you think I have missed anything I can include in later editions.

About me

I have been working, advising, lecturing, mentoring and writing within the education sector for many years, focusing on behaviour, classroom management, emotional and social intelligence and the role that brain maturation and cognitive development plays within this. Along with my wife Sonia who specialises in providing insight and strategies for SEND students (and who provided the input for the SEND section), I work with headteachers, teachers, NQTs, student teachers, teaching assistants (TAs), children, students and parents within every area of education. We meet and deal with an extensive range of issues present within secondary, primary and special schools as well as independent schools.

Belonging and respect

The problems schools are facing all fundamentally come down to the same thing: no matter what the situation, people want to be understood, listened to and valued. In short, they want to have a sense of belonging and to be respected. When people feel these things are absent then the reaction is seldom positive for themselves or those around them.

These are the foundational ingredients that make us a caring species, and this should be our approach with everyone that we come into contact with on a daily basis. But on top of this, all educators have a more important role to play as we engage with children and young people who are at crucial stages of their development. We have the power to influence how they view themselves, what they believe they can and cannot achieve, how they view others and the world, how they will manage their lives now and in their futures.

Parents and carers also play important role, but increasingly we within education are becoming an influential alternative adult in the lives of so many as we engage with them on a daily basis within our classrooms and schools. Children and young people bring their issues, needs and concerns to school and increasingly we are needing to be able to show, demonstrate, model the approaches that will enable them to cope and find their own strategies to manage their emotions, stresses and anxieties. We need to support them as well as to intervene on their behalf when appropriate. We are naive to think that we can now just be the providers of a curriculum and nothing else.

Therefore, it is crucial that we enable those who sit in front of us on a daily basis to grow into people who will make a positive contribution to the world in which they live and will become responsible for. When young people who I work with and help in their approach to life ask me, 'Why do you do this work?', I say 'Because one day you might come and live next door to me and I want nice neighbours!'

The rise in mental health issues and anxiety within the young and those attending university is proof enough that at present we are not getting it right and they have not learnt coping strategies to handle the stresses they experience. New Institute for Public Policy Research analysis (Thorley, 2017) found nearly *five times* as many students as ten years ago disclosed a mental health condition to their university.

In this book, I aim to explain what we can do that will make a difference and give those that we seek to care for the best possible lives that they can have: emotionally, socially, cognitively, and in terms of educational achievement. Thirty years after leaving university people won't be asking what degree and qualifications you obtained, but they will want to know about your life, and the values and attitude that you have towards the planet, others and yourself. This book will help you not only lay solid foundations for the children and young people you work with, but also gives insight as to why you are seeing some of the emotions and behaviour in front of you and what you will be able to do about it. It will also provide you with the basics of good practice to become the kind of teacher that they won't forget. I hope to show you that the young people in your schools and classes will appreciate you for the insights you can give, so that they will feel they belonged to you but that you also understood, listened to and valued them.

Some of the material in the book has been devised by myself and has proved effective; various other strategies are tried and tested common practice within educational establishments, but I have provided insight as to why I believe they work, and how they are affecting the students and children, so you not only know what to do but why it's important to do so.

In the meantime, enjoy being in the best profession in the world, remember why you wanted to go into teaching and hold that positive thought. Without you as a good teacher, there would be no doctors or lawyers or architects. And on that note, one of you will be teaching someone who will one day become the future Education Secretary. Please make sure you help them learn that care, understanding of others, and creating a *supportive*, inclusive environment where all can have a sense of belonging, is key for making teaching work, and only after those things have been established can you expect teachers as well as children and students to thrive. Enjoy the read!

Victor Allen

References

The Center for Generational Kinetics. (2018) *The State of Generation Z*. Austin, TX: The Center for Generational Kinetics. Available at: https://genhq.com/annual-gen-z-research-study/ (accessed 17 December 2019).

Thorley, C. (2017) *Not by Degrees: Improving Mental Health in the UK's Universities*. London: Institute for Public Policy Research. Available at: www.ippr.org/files/2017-09/1504645674_not-by-degrees-170905.pdf (accessed 17 December 2019).

PART 1

The brain

Chapter 1

The 3Ms and the BASE

Why are some teachers able to cope with all the stress and pressure of their job, while others fold under the same pressure and stress? What are the triggers for the stress? What might be the solution to coping effectively? In addressing these questions, throughout this book you will read about my views on the sense of coherence to help maintain a calm approach to life (the 3Ms) and also the BASE, creating the right environment to flourish. Here is a brief outline as to what I mean by those terms.

The 3Ms, also known as sense of coherence

The sense of coherence (SOC) concept was originated by Aaron Antonovsky in 1979 to explain why some people become ill under stress and others stay healthy. I was first introduced to this by my good friend Dietmar Seehuber, a psychiatrist and therapist working in Germany. When he explained Antonovsky's salutogenic approach to me, i.e. the search for the origins of health rather than the cause of disease, it made perfect sense to what I see and experience on a daily basis with adults and young people.

SOC is defined as 'The extent to which one has a pervasive, enduring though dynamic, feeling of confidence that one's environment is predictable and that things will work out as well as can reasonably be expected' in other words, it's a mixture of optimism and control – a great combination for any workplace and classroom (Collingwood, 2018).

Antonovsky named the three components of the SOC as comprehensibility, manageability and meaningfulness.

To make it easier to remember I changed comprehensibility into *Model*, so you now have 3Ms.

Comprehensibility (*Model*) is the extent to which events are perceived as making logical sense, that they are ordered, consistent and structured. So, in fact our mind has an order or Model into which everything fits and makes sense.

You can now understand why it is that children and students ask 'What are we going to do today?', and also why it is that when you are new to a school and you meet them for the first time you may be faced with some silly behaviour as they have become unsettled within their expected model. This sense of unsettlement can be caused by changes in the order of the day, holidays, weekends, sometimes when having to go to different parents or carers, the arrival of new students within the class, changes to the classroom, or anything that brings changes and with them uncertainty. The changes don't need to be negative to cause this uncertainty; they just need to be changes. Be aware of this and be prepared, as your emotional stability and calmness will help bring calmness back to them. The more you can prepare for any changes that you know are coming, the better for their immature brains to prepare.

Manageability is the extent to which a person feels they can cope or has the resources to enable them to cope.

Therefore, the very nature of your role as a teacher will impact on the manageability part of the 3Ms as you seek to challenge the students to try and learn new things which will bring with it the uncertainty of their ability to cope. If this feels debilitating for them, then they will find it hard to even try to attempt it. The answer is in how the brain tries to manage by looking for past skills or available resources for them to manage, and you will become the valuable resource within their lives as you extend their learning. Remember it is you as a resource which will make the task manageable, so when the person says 'I can't do this' instead of saying, 'Well, give it a go', or encouraging them just to have a try, you could say, 'That's fine – at the moment you on your own may not be able to do it, but I am here to help. Remember what my title is: Teacher! And I happen to be able not only to do it but I can help you to do it as well. Together we will learn.'

You don't need to say the whole speech, but you get my drift. Let them know you are here to help and make it manageable for them.

Meaningfulness is how much a person feels that life makes sense and challenges are worthy of commitment; that is, that their life, their work, is meaningful for them. This is the most important of the three as it has to be meaningful for them to even bother to attempt to learn to do something or try something. The meaningfulness has to be for the here and now, as well as also having to have some purpose in the future. For most children and young people the here and now are crucial for them to do something. Ask yourself, how you are you making the lessons meaningful? You can only truly know how to do that by knowing the children and students you wish to teach. If they ask the question, 'Why are we doing this?', your answer must meet *their* meaningfulness test as your idea of what is meaningful may not be the same as theirs. When children and students struggle in lessons, or socially or emotionally, we often find ways to make the issue more manageable and miss the most important part. Is it in fact meaningful to them to try or change their behaviour in the first place? No matter how much help you give someone, if it's not meaningful for them to try or conform to your expectations then they won't.

The question I believe our minds continually and constantly asks us is: are all of the 3Ms in line at this moment in time? For example:

Model: I understand what is happening now. I know what is happening next.

Manageable: I can manage, or I have the help necessary to manage the situation I am facing at this moment.

Meaningful: The time I am spending doing the thing I am engaged in is meaningful and I see the purpose for it.

(You can see how this fits neatly into the requirements of every child and student within your classroom as well as into everyday life as a whole.)

If the answer is yes, then you will be mentally OK and be able to relax and do your best. But if the answer to one or a combination of them is no then you will be starting the process of becoming stressed. Your emotional brain, along with other areas of the brain, will become triggered as it seeks to recall similar past experiences to find a suitable course of action to take, so you regain control or at least obtain some measure of understanding. During this process you will lose the ability to be working at your optimum.

If you start to feel anxiety within yourself, it will be because one or a combination of the three are not in line. The more you recognise this pattern within yourself and help to establish the pattern as best you can in others, then the less the stress will occur.

BASE: creating the right environment

The BASE describes the foundational aspects that every human needs to grow and develop emotionally and socially. It's an acronym, which stands for: Belonging, Autonomy, Social and Emotional competence. (See Deci and Ryan, 2000.)

Teachers should be able to meet their students' core psychological needs of belonging, autonomy, and social/emotional competence (also known as relatedness) and create interesting and challenging lessons that are relevant to their lives. Students should be given appropriate levels of challenges and they should be able to make decisions about their own learning. When they are faced with difficulties, the support system should be in place to help them. Through this process, students become more interested in learning. When teachers see motivated students, they too become more interested to teach (Wang, 2017).

I have been in thousands of classes across the country and every time I have seen disruptive students, I can guarantee that they don't feel a sense of belonging within the class they are being disruptive in. I have encouraged every teacher to first and foremost provide an environment where every student has a sense of belonging. Once that has been created then you encourage autonomy within that class, for both the learning as well as the behaviour. Both of those aspects require training, coaching and mentoring from a teacher or support worker. The end result is if a person feels they have autonomy then they will develop competent skills to manage themselves appropriately. The competence that they develop will be in their interaction with others socially and emotionally – thereby becoming more emotionally intelligent as well as more competent at managing tasks assigned to them by the teacher.

This BASE is the foundation that should weave itself throughout the school, department, classroom and environment. It should be the model for all work for both staff and students so that all can develop and grow.

In order for you to ascertain as quickly as possible which of the 3Ms is out of kilter, there are some very basic questions you can ask when having to talk with a child or students about their behaviour, or if you think something else is going on affecting their attention and you want to check how they are.

It also helps you keep a good relationship with them as you work on building and maintaining a good BASE for them. I encourage teachers to use the crib sheets on the following pages in every classroom with their students so, if extra support is needed, they are able to pass on some accurate information that can help with their work with the child or student.

References

Collingwood, J. (2018) 'Your Sense of Coherence', available at: https://psychcentral.com/lib/your-sense-of-coherence/ (accessed 18 December 2019).

Deci, E. L. and Ryan, R. M. (2000) 'The "What" and "Why" of Goal Pursuits: Human Needs and the Self-determination of Behaviour', *Psychological Inquiry*, 11(4), 227–268.

Wang, C. K. J. (2017) *The Joy of Learning: What It is and How to Achieve It*. Available at: http://merl.nie.edu.sg/documents/JoyofLearning.pdf (accessed 18 December 2019).

Talking with others

THE 3 Ms

Model – **Believing that things happen in an orderly and predictable fashion**

- FIRST – Check that everything in school is happening in the way the person expects.
- Once you have clarified this – ask how things are outside of school and their life in general.
- Is something happening to cause this person anxiety, which affects them managing their emotions within school?
- This provides you with an opportunity to get to know the person and their situation.
- **REMEMBER** – you might need to pass on some information they say, especially if it seems to be a child protection issue.

Manageable – **A belief in one's own ability to do what is being asked of them and that they have the support to accomplish it**

- Is what they are being asked to do within school/lesson, too hard or easy for them?
- Do they understand what they are being asked to do? Get them to explain to you.
- Do they have enough knowledge to help them complete the work which has been set for them?
- Is there anything else they would like to help them? **REMEMBER** you want them to build up their own ways to cope, so encourage them to find answers or understanding themselves.
- Find out if there is a situation they are facing outside of school with friends or family they are struggling with?

Meaningful – **Is it relevant, interesting and a source of satisfaction? Do they understand that there is a good reason to do it and also to care about the outcome?**

This is the most important of the 3Ms and you will need to ask the person so that you really try to GET TO KNOW THEM:

- Do you know why you are doing what you have been asked to do?
- What do you like in life?
- Who do you like and why?
- What do you like most about your friends?
- What is the best thing about you?
- What do you want to do in life?
- What do you value in life?

In light of what they have said, how can what they are being asked to do work alongside their own values or interests? How can they make it meaningful?

Talking with others

BASE: BELONGING, AUTONOMY, SELF ESTEEM

Listen well!

Needs of people when they talk to you

- To be recognised and remembered
- Valued
- Appreciated
- Respected
- Understood/comfortable with you, they feel they can share a want or a need.

Remember that your tone of voice will influence the conversation.

Your Approach

- Ask questions to help them factually explain their want or need to you.
- What is their present situation? How would they like the situation to be? What is the obstacle keeping them from the desired situation?
- Help them to focus on things they can do. Does the best solution link with their life's goals and values?
- **REMEMBER.** Provide them with an opportunity to demonstrate their social and emotional competence, autonomy, maintain their self-esteem and sense of belonging. Problems are often learning tools for life.
- Look for inconsistencies in what they want and what they are achieving.
- Highlight an alternative and offer it to them.
- Continually be aware of your emotions/tone of voice/body language.
- Remember the 60 sec. interview technique to try to shift their brain management if being too emotional which prevents clear thought (*Fish & chips*).
- Clarify the 3Ms (Model, Manageable, Meaningful).
- Stay calm – learn from the experience.

'May your patience always be with you'

Chapter 2

An introduction to brain maturation

The increases in knowledge we have gained since the 1980s regarding brain development are in part due to advancements in magnetic resonance imaging (MRI), which uses strong magnetic fields and radio waves to produce detailed images of the inside of the brain. Since the 1990s, functional magnetic resonance imaging (fMRI) has measured brain activity by detecting changes associated with blood flow. To put it very simply, when an area of the brain is in use, blood flow to that region increases. So, we can now watch the brain in operation.

This has led to a greater understanding of not only how the brain works but also the developmental stages associated with brain growth. This is particularly useful for all those teaching children and young adults. We now understand that the brain is fully mature by the time we reach our mid-twenties, with many remarkable significant changes taking place over this time. We also know the significant times when the brain is at its optimum level for learning new skills, such as languages and music. Typically, these events are best learnt as early as possible, which means the brain of a teenager is far less able to learn a language than say a 2-year-old. We also realise that adolescence plays a part in how the brain views the world, which goes some way to explaining why teenagers take far more risks during this period. I often say to teenagers 'I haven't met many 50-year-old joy riders!'

The brain also maintains its efficiency by pruning rarely used synapses. Synapses are brain structures that allow the neurons to transmit an electrical or chemical signal to another neuron. There are significant points at which this takes place, specifically around the ages of 2 and 16. This process also occurs to a lesser extent continually. Basically, every time you do something, learn something, remember something, your brain is either creating a new connection or using old ones. If you don't use those connectional pathways very often your brain has a handy way of getting rid of them altogether, which explains why when shown how to use a white board, if you don't use it again for a year you have forgotten how to – or rather your brain has done away with those pathways as you didn't keep using them. It's your brain's way of maintaining more efficient brain function as we get older and learn more complex information. Constant stimulus causes synapses to grow and become permanent. If you don't use it you will lose it!

The tables at the end of the chapter (see Tables 2.1 and 2.2) illustrate that development, looking at all the key stages through school life highlighting specific things to be aware of that might help explain why you see situations in front of you.

Table 2.1 Brain Development: Primary School Guide

		Primary School Guide Key Stage 1	
Approximate Ages Corresponding stages	Reception Infant/Toddler 2–4	Year 1 Child 5–6	Year 2 Child 6–7
Brain Development	Age 3, the brain is 80% adult size. By age 3 80% of synaptic connections are made. Early experiences are crucial. Long term memory is developing. Good nutritional food important for brain development.	Limbic system developing, including the amygdala (emotions), hippocampus (memory). Not yet able to have reasoned reactions to everyday situations, but watching and learning from adults. Their early emotional experiences become embedded in their brain and can influence them as adults.	Limbic system still developing. The brain is now 95% adult size. Will be remembering how people treat them and the emotions associated with it. They always want to be right!
Mental and Intellectual Development	Large strides in language development. Provide hands on activities to explore through their five senses. They will say 'I do it' and want to make choices. Learning about and experiencing their emotions.	Dressing themselves and communicating in sentences. The more experiences they have, the more they learn. They have no filters so they absorb everything.	Development of logic, can approach a problem and consider various outcomes, learning to organize their thoughts. Will ask more questions to gain understanding.
Interpersonal Development	Important to have secure attachments. Ask them 'How do they think others are feeling' when something happens to help gain emotional understanding of others.	Getting along with others and understanding fairness and their place in the world. Learning how to control their behaviour.	Enjoying being with peers more, yet prefer own gender. It is either right or wrong. No grey areas. Start to have best friends. May have difficulty getting along with other children.
Adult Support and Guidance	High exposure to experiences and activities. Keep them moving as this is good for them and the brain as it increases heart rate, blood flow and oxygen to the brain. Read stories to them. Be intune with their emotions and build a sense of belonging.	Imaginative play. Read regularly with them. Keep active. Be understanding and tolerant. They are learning about so many things and won't always make the right choice or do the right thing. Maintain their self-esteem and confidence when dealing with them when they don't get it right. Continue to affirm their sense of belonging and increase their autonomy.	Involve them in jobs at school and home. Help them develop routines and working with others. Develop leadership duties in school. Continue to affirm their sense of belonging and increase their autonomy as they start to make choices suited to an adult life.

	Year 3 Child 7–8	Year 4 Early Adolescent 8–9	Year 5 Early Adolescent 9–10	Year 6 Early Adolescent 10–11
Approximate Ages Corresponding stages				
Brain Development	Becoming more cognitively flexible engaging in complex thinking and planning. Neural connections in the brain are being fine-tuned through pruning, Increase the brain's processing speed and efficiency.	Information travels with greater speed through the nervous system and different parts of the brain begin to work in coordination with one another in new combinations.	Differences start to emerge regarding maturity between boys and girls. Thesub-cortex will start the pruning earlier in girls as they start to become socially aware and mature.	Last great pruning of the brain. As children, we overproduce the connections – synapses – between brain cells. During puberty the body carries out a kind of topiary, snipping away some synapses while allowing others to strengthen. Over a few years, the number of synapses roughly halves, and the adult brain emerges.
Mental and Intellectual Development	Longer attention span meaning they able to manage less detailed direction. They like to share their knowledge with others. Improving literacy skills. Can utilize increasingly complex and creative strategies. Learning takes place most effectively through play experiences.	Their ability to apply logic and reason increases, as does their ability to focus attention. They are able to concentrate on tasks for longer periods of time and begin to use their own resources prior to seeking adult help or they may seek out peers for assistance. 8-year-olds demonstrate more highly-developed thinking skills as well as the ability to solve problems with creative strategies.	Attention span up to an hour or more. They enjoy doing research on topics of interest to them. Work well in groups and cooperate to work on projects or activities.	Learning accelerates significantly during this period and they are able to tackle more complex material in maths, English and other subjects. Increasing ability to expand upon logic and abstract thinking yet they can lose this ability under stress (such as tests) and revert back to concrete solutions. Increasingly self-aware in terms of knowing their own feelings, needs and world view. Children therefore find it harder to respond positively to being ordered around.

Primary School Guide Key Stage 2

(continued)

Table 2.1 Brain Development: Primary School Guide (*Continued*)

	Primary School Guide Key Stage 2			
Approximate Ages Corresponding stages	Year 3 Child 7–8	Year 4 Early Adolescent 8–9	Year 5 Early Adolescent 9–10	Year 6 Early Adolescent 10–11
Interpersonal Development	More independent and are sociable. May have spells of being rebellious and aggressive. Be the role model for them when dealing with emotions.	Begin to understand the concept of masking emotions and can vary their use of coping strategies to deal with challenging situations. In peer interactions, they may start to engage in leadership, goal-setting, elaborate fantasy play and an assortment of interactive games. Having one close friend is a key developmental accomplishment at this age.	It becomes emotionally more important to have friends, especially of the same sex. They become more aware of changes to their body and their self-image.	At this age they start thinking and sounding almost 'grown-up' and have the language and cognitive ability to gather information and formulate well-organised opinions and thoughts. They will also be learning how to tackle negative peer pressure if self-esteem is strong. This period starts the bridge between child and emerging adult.
Adult Support and Guidance	Encourage physical activity, children mature quicker if they engage in physical activity. Focus on strengths, abilities and talents, Help them to start to manage their emotions and be comfortable with them. Increase their ability to manage aspects of their lives i.e. remembering things to do that make their lives easier.	They now read for pleasure with books associated to their interests. May want to rely less on adult supervision yet be aware of them sharing their needs and wants. Increase encouraging them to find ways to solve emotional and social problems. Online activities should be restricted, with none before bed time.	Children who feel good about themselves can resist peer pressure more, so keep developing their sense of self-worth. Talk about their friends and the challenges they are facing and help them develop strategies. On line activities should be restricted, with none before bed time.	Provide them with time to play and express their childishness as well as engaging them in discussion about friends, society as well as world issues as their interest will be developing on all fronts. Look to encourage more autonomy regarding social and emotional interaction as you encourage development towards adulthood.

Table 2.2 Brain Development: Secondary School Guide

	Secondary School Guide Key Stages 3 and 4				
Approximate Ages Corresponding stages	Year 7 Early Adolescent 11–12	Year 8 Mid Adolescent 12–13	Year 9 Mid Adolescent 13–14	Year 10 Late Teens 14–15	Year 11 Late Teens 15–16
Brain Development	Adolescence is a time characterised by change – hormonally, physically, psychologically, and socially. They are now entering into the last period of major changes in the brain. In the frontal cortex, gray matter volumes peak at approximately 11 years of age in girls and 12 years of age in boys. Subsequently, rarely used connections are selectively pruned.	They rely heavily on the emotional regions of their brains. It can be challenging to make what adults consider logical and appropriate decisions, *Prospective memory* is a form of *memory* that involves remembering to perform a planned action or recalling a planned intention at some future point in time. However, between the ages of 10 and 14, *there was no significant change in performance.*	Because the prefrontal cortex is still developing, teenagers might rely on a part of the brain called the amygdala to make decisions and solve problems more than adults do. The amygdala is associated with emotions, impulses, aggression and instinctive behaviour.	At the age of 15 years, there is little difference in adolescents' and adults' decision-making patterns pertaining to hypothetical situations. Teens were found to be capable of reasoning about the possible harm or benefits of different courses of action. However, in the real world, teens still engaged in dangerous behaviours, despite understanding the risks involved.	The front part of the brain, the prefrontal cortex, is remodelled last. The prefrontal cortex is the decision-making part of the brain, responsible for the child's ability to plan and think about the consequences of actions, solve problems and control impulses. Changes in this part continue into early adulthood. The prefrontal cortex of a 15-year-old is very different from that of a 30-year-old, both physically and in how it's used.

(continued)

Table 2.2 Brain Development: Secondary School Guide (*Continued*)

	Secondary School Guide Key Stages 3 and 4				
Approximate Ages Corresponding stages	Year 7 Early Adolescent 11–12	Year 8 Mid Adolescent 12–13	Year 9 Mid Adolescent 13–14	Year 10 Late Teens 14–15	Year 11 Late Teens 15–16
Mental and Intellectual Development	At 12 years, adolescents decrease their reliance on concrete thinking and begin to show the capacity for abstract thinking, visualisation of potential outcomes, and a logical understanding of cause and effect.	Some adolescents may be able to apply logical operations to school work long before they are able to apply them to personal dilemmas. When emotional issues arise, they often interfere with an adolescent's ability to think in more complex ways. The ability to consider possibilities, as well as facts, may influence decision-making, in either positive or negative ways.	Can display an awareness of thinking (they understand the task being tried and are able to select strategies to succeed), and an awareness of thinking strategies (they are able to self-assess, ask themselves questions, revise their thinking, and direct their own learning). Support this development by modelling your own thinking and problem solving aloud! Scaffold their thinking by helping them to notice their own strategies and discovering together if they used words or did not, if they are worth retaining or if new strategies are necessary.	The middle adolescent often questions more extensively and analyses more extensively. Thinks about and begins to form his or her own code of ethics (for example, 'What do I think is right?'). They think about different possibilities and begin to develop their own identity (for example, 'Who am I?'). They think about and begin to systematically consider possible future goals (for example, 'What do I want?') and begin to make his or her own plans. Able to think long-term.	Because older teenagers are more intellectually advanced than a child or younger teens, adults can have more back-and-forth conversations with them. They're better able to understand other people's points of views, and they're more open to other perspectives and ideas. Many older teenagers will use their new intellectual capacities as 'logical weapons' against their parents. This has more to do with them separating from you. They'll punch holes in your logic, and they'll challenge you with thought-out reason.

	Secondary School Guide Key Stages 3 and 4				
Approximate Ages Corresponding stages	Year 7 Early Adolescent 11–12	Year 8 Mid Adolescent 12–13	Year 9 Mid Adolescent 13–14	Year 10 Late Teens 14–15	Year 11 Late Teens 15–16
Interpersonal Development	Rely more on the emotional region of their brains when reading the emotions of others, which is more impulsive when compared to a logical or measured interpretation, so they often misread other people's emotions. Boys especially misread and tend to think it is anger. They are searching to identify who they are and often use pop culture to define themselves.	Early teen years, adolescent egocentrism emerges. Adolescent egocentrism is the belief that others are highly invested in and attentive to their appearance and actions (imaginary audience) and that their experiences and emotions are unique and known only to and by them (personal fable). Egocentrism at this age is the root of self-consciousness, and it also fuels the teen's sense of themselves as uniquely powerful and invincible. While a tween or teen realizes other people have different points of view (in contrast to the preschooler who displays egocentrism), they use that knowledge to become preoccupied with other people's perceptions of them.	Uncertain, unhappy and sensitive; withdrawn; spend a lot of time alone; need privacy; convinced that everyone else is watching and judging; very concerned with body image and self-esteem is at a low ebb; not sociable with adults; friendships tend to be group-focused; more squabbling than a year ago.	The middle adolescent's use of systematic thinking begins to influence relationships with others. Still can have a tendency to return to childish behaviour. Peer group influences interests and clothing styles.	Even though they have a certain amount of empathy and can understand that others have different ideas, they often strongly believe that their own ideas are the most true. *Emotional and social development.* Much of teens' emotional and social growth is about finding their place in the world. They are trying to figure out 'Who am I?' and 'How do I fit in?' So it is normal for their emotions to change from day to day.

(continued)

Table 2.2 Brain Development: Secondary School Guide (*Continued*)

	Secondary School Guide Key Stages 3 and 4				
Approximate Ages Corresponding stages	Year 7 Early Adolescent 11–12	Year 8 Mid Adolescent 12–13	Year 9 Mid Adolescent 13–14	Year 10 Late Teens 14–15	Year 11 Late Teens 15–16
Adult Guidance and Support	To counteract their rebellious nature at this age find ways to offer them opportunities to make decisions. For example, ask them to write down 'Things I think I can do alone now', go over them and choose together. Talk through decisions step by step with your child. Ask about possible courses of action your child might choose and talk through potential consequences. Encourage your child to weigh up positive consequences or rewards against negative ones.	Adolescents should not be overprotected, but be allowed to make mistakes, learn from their own experiences, and practice self-regulation. Parents and teachers can help adolescents through this period by listening and offering support and guidance. Let your child take some healthy risks. New and different experiences help them develop an independent identity, explore grow-up behaviour and move towards independence. Try to match your language level to the level of your child's understanding. For important information, you can check their understanding by asking them to tell you in their own words what they have just heard.	Help your child find new creative and expressive outlets for their feelings. They might be expressing and trying to control new emotions. Many teenagers find that doing or watching sport or music, writing and other art forms are good outlets.	Include them in discussions about a variety of topics, issues, and current events. To share ideas and thoughts with you. To think independently and develop their own ideas especially in setting their own goals. Stimulate them to think about possibilities for the future. Compliment and praise them for well-thought-out decisions. Assist them in re-evaluating poorly made decisions for themselves.	With the increasing demands of school and social life, teenagers often do not get the eight to 10 hours of sleep they need each night. Encourage them to make sleep a priority, and try to help eliminate obstacles to getting a good night of sleep (such as mobilephone use, watching television and using the computer when trying to go to sleep).

The first few years of life are crucial for the young person, as they experience all that life has to offer them. At this stage the brain is very much like a blank canvas on which we can help paint a picture of the world. Within the brain there are already a number of hard-wired reactions that have taken hundreds of thousands of years to embed. These are designed to keep us safe during times of danger and anxiety: Fight, Flight, Flock, or Freeze. On top of these we need to build skills necessary to interact emotionally and socially with others. These skills are learnt through the two-way process of the child interacting with a parent or caregiver, who gives them the loving attention needed to feel safe and cared for.

You will see the natural responses to stress played out during your time in school. Angry and arguing students and children (fight), absenteeism and absconding from lessons (flight), groups of students messing about together (flock), and those who seem unable to communicate with you and shut down (freeze). That sense of belonging will be key throughout life, and children and young people will constantly refer back mentally to these early experiences throughout their lives. So, if those experiences have been positive, helping the brain make connections needed to develop self-regulation, motivation, communication and a sense of self-worth, then this will help the young person to develop into a healthy capable adult. Yet we know that not all childhoods are like that, and that unfortunately some children face adverse childhood experiences (ACEs) which contribute to making the start in life negative. We also know that exposure to family violence, poverty, or anything that prevents access to quality early learning experiences, can negatively impact a child's brain development and long-term success.

So poor behaviour may not just be a reaction to what you have asked them to do, rather it could in some way have triggered an emotional memory associated with an adverse experience. The emotional reaction they demonstrate may be more a reflection upon them, and possibly their early lives, rather than on you as a teacher.

From the age of three and a half, when we start to develop long term memory within the hippocampus, emotions are associated with those memories through our amygdala.

It is key for us as adults to realise that we, through our interaction, will be making life-long memories and impressions on the young people we come into contact with. I remember someone saying that the role of an adult is to provide young people with memories. Make sure yours are worth keeping! These experiences are not just events that happened to us but are the material which we use to shape our identity and our self. I am sure you can appreciate that when a child's early experiences have not been positive then they need to re-evaluate, and will also need help in choosing a different way of learning how to respond to them.

Each young person within your classroom is not just learning the subject that you are teaching but is also learning from the experiences that you are providing. Each young person is also making assessments about their experiences which will become foundational within their lives. The role of teachers to help provide emotionally stable, nurturing, fulfilling experience has never been so important. Whereas previously children would have learned emotional and social skills through imaginary, unorganised unstructured play, now they learn through interaction on tablets and phones or overseen by adults in organised events, a process which ill prepares them for the social and emotional intricacies of the world. The brain is going to develop successfully when it is nourished, motivated towards action and learning and encouraged to experience new things. We, as a species, learn from our mistakes and we, as teachers, will experience lots and lots of mistakes from those we are aiming to teach. Each mistake is a learning opportunity, be it a mistake in a formal lesson or a mistake within the choices we make in life. From the position of a teacher, these represent an opportunity for you to influence how the brain learns from experience.

PART 2

General strategies for working in primary and secondary schools

Strategies for making a good first impression and getting the best out of parents and fellow staff members

It is very helpful, when dealing with others, to appreciate that decisions made and approaches taken are not solely based on an evaluation of a situation we are confronted with or need to address but will also have been affected by a variety of different influences during our lives. These influences will include: how we feel; what information we have; the comments of others; what our values are; the society in which we live; our parents or carers; our early years; the love (or lack of it) we received; how we are cared for by others; our personality type; genes; health; the amount of sleep we have had, or the lack of it; the amount of energy we have to cope within any situation; our friends; our family; the environment we grew up in; and the role models we will have had. All of the above influences and more can and do make a difference in our lives and the choices we make. We often like to think we are in control, yet on a daily basis the external and sometimes internal influences impact on the choices we make, sometimes within a fraction of a second. So, your colleagues, parents and various other people that you meet are often reacting and relating to you through all these things just as you are with them. So, if it's not what you like, or what you expected, react like Abraham Lincoln who said, 'I don't like that man, I must get to know him better.'

First impressions

With this in mind, when working with others we should recognise that first impressions or quick evaluations of people can often be wrong. It takes just a few milliseconds to form an opinion of someone. We know that you should never judge a book by its cover, but try telling your hard-wired brain that. Researchers found evidence that a single glance at a person's face for just 33 to 100ms was sufficient to form a first impression (South Palomares and

Young, 2017). So, first impressions for the classroom, parents and colleagues matter. Think about what impressions you wish to make and dress and act accordingly. I am often surprised that the first thought that goes through teachers' minds when they get dressed in the morning is, 'How comfortable will I be in this?' rather than 'What impression do I wish to make and how comfortable will I be?' For some the dress code seems to be one of what they have always worn, but I want to encourage you to think about the impact you are wanting to have on those you are going to be talking to, because believe me you will be making an impression. How often do you start watching a programme on the TV, whether it be news, current affairs or anything else, and you share the comment with your partner, 'Look at what they are wearing!' Well, the same thought will be going through those you meet today. So, in your interaction with others, start by dressing for the part. I once heard a dress code for teachers wonderfully explained for new female teachers by another female colleague: 'I don't want to look down it, up it or through it!'

In those milliseconds on first seeing people, the brain is operating to ascertain if that person is trustworthy and competent, so dress accordingly. Iron your clothes, wear clothing that fits, and shoes that still look pristine even if they are a few years old. You are showing that you have a duty of care and that starts with yourself. If you do wear the same outfit every day, you can look to personalise your own style by adding some variation. Find out if the school has a dress code, and if in doubt go for quality over quantity.

Colleagues

Meeting, working, sharing and cooperating with your colleagues will become the number one activity alongside your teaching and involvement with children and students. A lot of the people you will meet will be pleased to see you and have you as part of the team, but others will often be wrapped up in their own work and life and not realise you are there. Schools are remarkable places, working for the same end yet often not working and cooperating collaboratively together. The proximity of staffrooms, classrooms and faculty offices often make meeting others not in your area awkward. Sometimes you will only get to see other members of staff if your school has a staff briefing once a week, which does little to build up the sense of belonging and team commitment needed in such a pressured environment. Yet you will be able to learn a lot from these colleagues, as well as collaborating with them regarding some of the trickier members of the student population.

Therefore, do as much as you can to build relationships not only with your immediate colleagues but with others around the school, especially those who will be able to make your life easier, such as the maintenance crew and IT department. Photographs of teaching and support staff will help you put names to faces.

The designated special educational needs person (the SENDCO) will be able to provide as much information and advice as appropriate to help you regarding the special needs of specific children within your classroom.

All these people help make the school run effectively and efficiently and working with them and learning from them will help improve your knowledge, understanding and skill level.

Communication

Emails are the main mode of communication within schools and I spend a lot of my time encouraging teachers not to send them to colleagues when a quick chat can suffice, as well as being often far more effective. The personal time when taken to explain, ask, inform on a one to one basis with eye contact goes a long way to building relationships and avoiding misunderstandings. Remember with those personal interactions, your body language and tone of voice will also make an impact.

It is important to remember that there is no throwaway moment when dealing with others, especially colleagues – every interaction counts. I remember a conversation between two colleagues which impacted their relationship for years. It all started when one made a joke about the other whilst introducing him to someone else. He said, 'Ever since you said that I have never worked well with you.'

The school is full of experience and expertise. I have never met a teacher yet who doesn't have some tip that is worth listening to. It's not just the students and young people that are learning. Pooling of ideas, working smart and finding ways to still tick the boxes all help you to be able to spend more time in the work you enjoy, teaching. Your colleagues will know strategies and the best way to stay mentally secure within the school is to talk with them, share and ask for advice in situations you come across.

Parents

When dealing with parents remember they went to school as well, so bear in mind that they will view schools through their own experiences. As you can appreciate, not all of those experiences will have been good ones. Parents may be far more used to talking with a headteacher than you are, because of the many times they had to do so because of their own behaviour in the past.

Whatever their experience, you are there to make sure that from now on it is going to be as supportive and as cooperative as possible. Get to know the parents of your students as soon as you can. Your colleagues will be very keen to tell you which parents are cooperative and those who are particularly negative or hard work. Don't be influenced by this opinion; it is your role to build the best possible relationship and sometimes this may require more work. But the same approach that applies to children and young people also applies to adults – they want to be listened to, feel valued and appreciated. They may well be making an assumption of you based upon past experiences and sometimes this has to be overcome before the relationship moves forward, so be consistent with your approach with them. Ask them about their own experience of school to help you gauge how they view school now. Ask about their hopes and aspirations relating to their child and see what you can do to help make this a reality. Try to make calling home as much as you can about positive aspects of their child's behaviour as well as their academic success. Try to call home to introduce yourself if you can, so that for all parents the first time they hear from you will be on good terms.

You can share with them the information contained within this book relating to brain development. These stages will inevitably mean that their child's behaviour will also change, and this can at times become a source of conflict or confusion as the young person struggles to find their own identity and place within the adult world. Find out as much as you can about home life without being too intrusive, just so that you can build up a picture of what is happening within the child's everyday experiences that could possibly impact upon their behaviour in school. The role you are playing as an alternative adult within the life of the child or young person needs to be as collaborative as possible with their parents. It is often a combined experience that helps nurture the child through the stresses of life. Often the lives that children and young people are experiencing bear no reflection upon the lives and experiences of those who are employed to teach them, so the more that you can find out will widen your own skills and understanding.

Points to remember when making a phone call home

Prepare for the call

This means taking into account the person you are going to be speaking to and could be as basic as finding out what is their understanding of English. Have they had other calls in relation to the one you are making? Have you got all the information relevant for the conversation? Do you know what you want the outcome for the call to be? This will help in your assessment of how successful the call has been. Try to find a time to make the call when you can be private and not disturbed.

During the call

The other person has no non-verbal clues, but will pick up on your tone as well as whether you are smiling when you start the conversation and the mood that you are in. So be aware of the message you are conveying through your tone. Avoid boredom, as in, 'Yes I am making the same call for the 50th time and it has now lost all meaning to me.' And try not to give the impression that you are in a hurry, especially if you are the one that made the call and instigated the conversation. They won't be able to see you so make sure that your tone matches the message as much as possible.

Listen

Calls are a two-way process so make sure you listen to what they are saying. They may give you some hints regarding other issues that may be taking place and could prove important, so give them time to speak, and listen. Repeat back the information they are giving to you to clarify that you have the facts straight.

Speak clearly

For some people to have a call from school and a teacher is a highly significant event and often the caller will need to repeat what you are saying to a partner so make sure that you are clear and precise about what you want to say.

Clarify

This means making sure that you question anything that you are unsure about, as well as to make sure that the other person has clarity regarding what has been said. Ask them if there is anything they are unsure about regarding what you have said.

Undivided attention

We all like to think we can multi-task, but what this truly means is we can do a surprising number of things at the same time very poorly. Stay focused on the one thing.

Cut off point

You may have instigated the call and have something specific that you wish to say but sometimes this can also trigger the parent or carer to raise other issues with you and you may find yourself no longer in control of the call as the parent wants to talk and talk. I have had teachers say to me, 'I just couldn't get them to stop talking.' If this happens and you wish to hear what they are saying but have no time at the moment, then you can say, 'Thank you for informing me about that, I really do want to hear more. I just wish I had time now. Can we arrange a better time for both of us when I don't have to be off to another meeting?' Remember, though, to repeat your initial message to make sure it didn't get lost in the comments from them at the end.

Alternatively, at the start of the call, if you know they are likely to talk a great deal and it's just not appropriate at that time, let them know right from the start that this is just a quick call as you only have ten minutes to pass on this piece of information. Remember to provide them with the alternative of another call when you know you will have more time. You can then ask them how long do they think they will need? This way you at least have some idea of the length and can hold them to it.

Sum up

Whatever the message, the call needs to end with a relationship that is intact and positive. This can often prove tricky, but the relationship is key for moving things forward in a positive manner, so the aim should always be to do that. The more calls that contain the ingredients of positivity means that when a more negative call has to be made enough credit has been banked and good will established that they know that your intention is always to make things better and work with them for the benefit of the child. Clarify any points. Let them know any steps you are going to take and make sure you do them within the prescribed time scale. Only promise things that you can do. If a follow up call is needed, then set time for that. Become a person that can be relied upon. Set reminders for yourself.

Leaving a message

If you have to leave a message, keep it short and to the point, highlighting what it is you wish to talk to them about and when is the best time to contact you. Let them know also that you will try to reach them again and when you will do so. Your tone of voice will be key to how they interpret what you are saying when leaving a message.

Your skill in people management will grow the more people you interact with. They will never cease to surprise you, disappoint you, challenge you and make you reflect upon yourself. To say, 'I will treat people as I want to be treated' will only leave you disappointed, missing out on lots of folks who are not like you. They may have a different viewpoint and different values to you and interpret words and sentences differently to you because of all the things I mentioned at the beginning. However you are treated or spoken to, politely or rudely, I would encourage you to stay true to yourself and your values and don't let the poor behaviour of others lead you to become someone who is also rude or vindictive. The chances are that rudeness, be it from a child or an adult, stems from them not being able to cope with the situation that they find themselves in. You can become someone who helps them learn to cope. As I often say to people 'May your patience always be with you.'

References

South Palomares, J. K. and Young, A. W. (2017) 'Facial First Impressions of Partner Preference Traits: Trustworthiness, Status and Attractiveness', *Social Psychological and Personality Science*, 9(8), 990–1000.

Chapter 4

Strategies for the start of the year or for a new class

The teaching profession is one of the best I know for fresh starts. Each September starts with teacher training days where the past year is scrutinised and the new year is mapped out, with changes and improvements being suggested from lessons learnt, new staff welcomed, and new priorities outlined. The students start afresh with an advancement in their year group and a fresh set of challenges.

It reminds me of the football league. Every year brings new players and fresh expectations, and sometimes new managers with new strategies. Everyone wants to do the best for the fans and each other, and all are hoping to advance upon the results of the previous year. It takes time for new players in a team, no matter what their skills, to embed themselves within the team and learn about each other. It's just the same for you and the students and children you are seeking to lead, coach mentor and teach.

The added luxury the teaching profession has is that it can also introduce milestones along the way through the year, with half terms and even the start of the calendar year, in January, offering themselves as suitable times to reflect over the previous weeks as well as setting new expectations and targets for the coming weeks. Take advantage of these opportunities by issuing those new expectations every time students and children return from breaks. You can also use these opportunities to explore the lessons learned both academically and socially, to evaluate what you have done and how things are progressing. It is vital to make a good start so as to build upon it. There is only one first impression so you might as well do what you can to get it right.

Getting the start right from the very beginning

As we saw in the previous chapter, first impressions do matter. Before you meet a new class, think about the impression you wish to make on the students and children when they first meet you. Think about how you will address them, what words you will use, what vision you will set out, and also your own expectations. These will become the words that they will remember as they return to you through the weeks that follow. Make sure that your words are both encouraging and personal to them. Include your desire for them to succeed with you and how you are looking forward to getting to know them. It would be good to ask who enjoys the subject and who struggles with it. This will not only demonstrate their willingness to share but will also show you who is the natural class leader and who are the followers. Inform them of your confidence and skill in being a teacher capable of making the lessons interesting and challenging and most of all relevant to them. You are seeking to create in their minds your intention that you intend to work with them on their success over the coming year.

Social classroom etiquette can be discussed based upon the students' age and understanding. Some people like to establish rules at the start of the year as a means to control and set social expectations. I prefer to use the time to set classroom expectations on behaviour as a means to help them develop their own social awareness of the needs of others and the best way to adapt to having to work in a group. For example:

- Talk about how they think you should get the class as a whole to be quiet when you need to say something.
- Give them examples of what others do and ask what they think is appropriate for them.
- Practise this throughout the lesson so that it becomes the norm.
- Help them to take charge of encouraging their friends to listen.
- Discuss the working environment needed for when working individually and also in small groups.
- Help them to develop the skill of being socially and emotionally aware of others.

You may find that some in your group will struggle with this, and they may need more help. This is the same process of differentiation that you would use in managing learning in your subject, it is just that the subject being taught is etiquette, manners and being respectful of others. For some who are also used to being told off and warned that if they continue it will result in a sanction, they will find it tricky to adjust, as they have got used to the telling off as the trigger for behaving. What you will be asking them to do is to self-regulate. This will require patience and persistence until they get the hang of it. But after a few weeks of reminding them at the start of the lesson what you are expecting and praising them for how much they are improving – as they will – you will see how this is helping them develop.

From the outset you will need to highlight that your classroom is a working environment and there are expectations placed upon you as an employee and on them as students. I am often surprised that some teachers forget how important this moment is in creating the right environment. This is your chance to impress upon them what you are hoping to achieve with their help and cooperation. Once that has been done then you should be spending time during the start of the year to get this good working relationship going.

Your relationship with your students' needs to become a partnership of expectations. You will be supplying the leadership, direction and learning, and they will be supplying their concentration, respect and cooperation so that you all can benefit from the time together. This will be easier for some than for others but that is where all the strategies in this book will come in to help you find the best approaches to help them get it right.

Getting to know who is in your class is vital. You will already have a list of names; expand on that by encouraging them to share information about themselves, such as their interests, hobbies, things they are good at, if they have any pets, or any brothers or sisters. Some teachers start with two truths and a lie about themselves and ask the students to guess which is which. There are many starter activities and I would recommend that you start with them in a new class when you meet for the first time. Start as you mean to go on with your approach. An excellent way of helping them understand your expectations as well as providing them with an opportunity of autonomy when it comes to classroom rules is to ask them all to come up with a list of zero tolerance things that should not take place within the classroom. Provide them all with an A to Z list and ask them to find a behaviour which they think should not be tolerated, to match each letter of the alphabet. Here are a few examples:

A	Arguing back
B	Bickering/bullying
C	Chatting/chewing gum/complaining
D	Doodling
E	Eating
F	No F word
G	Graffiti
H	Hollering
I	Interrupting
J	Jumping
K	Kicking
L	Littering
M	Marking
N	Nonsense
O	Offensive language
P	Play fighting
Q	Quarrelling
R	Rudeness
S	Swear words
T	Teasing
U	Unkind words
V	Vandalism
W	Winding people up
XYZ	Yelling

That first meeting will also highlight to you the emotional and social competence of some of the students – some will warm to you straight away and some will be more reserved or reticent. You have to remember that time and your consistency will be the things that make the most impressions. You cannot sow and harvest at the same time; like a farmer you need patience. Think about what you want to achieve with them by half term and then after the first term. Outline to them what it is that you are most wanting to see from them, socially and emotionally as well as academically. Let them know that you are interested in them all as people first and foremost, and the teaching that you will provide is just one aspect of all that you will learn together.

When you have been with them a few weeks you can do a simple exercise by asking them what was their first impression of you, and has it changed at all? This will give you an indication of whether you have achieved what you set out to do or if you need to perhaps alter your approach next time.

Start of the lesson each week

Being at the door at the start of the lesson ready for the students sets a good example. If, for whatever reason, you are unable to arrive before them then at the earliest opportunity when you have established them in the classroom, ask them what they think would be the best thing for them to do if they arrive and you are not there. A few minutes taken to establish this point will save you a lot of time in the future.

Talk through their suggestions with them until you arrive at one that you know is best for them, the school, and for you. This will involve them taking some responsibility for their own conduct and behaviour and also provides them with the opportunity to demonstrate to you their maturity, or lack of it in some cases.

Being there at the start is a good way to establish that the room is yours and they are your guests in your room and should act accordingly.

Having them line up outside is often a favourite method in schools to help the students calm down after perhaps the rush and play of the walk to the class.

Make sure that your welcome is encouraging and personal to them. Mentioning names and remembering things they may have mentioned to you or good things you have heard all make an impression. How you stand and the tone is all being observed by the students and can go a long way to creating a calm atmosphere.

If you have established a good routine and you have never been late, I would still advise at some point going through with them what they should do if you are late. Any opportunity for them to demonstrate to you good behaviour should be encouraged and built upon. The more you control them, then the less equipped they will be when you are absent.

Meeting at the door will also give you an opportunity to check the staple school necessities of uniform and dress code, earrings, make up etc. These can be addressed before entering into the classroom. Always do so in an encouraging manner. Students are skilled in the art of excuses, and you will need to have your own strategy for dealing with the infringements you have in front of you. I like to always make sure the onus is on the students to explain what they are going to do about the issue to make sure it doesn't occur again. Agree with them if you like their idea but always add that if it doesn't work then perhaps you both may need to have a talk together to come up with a better plan that will succeed. Add that you will see how they are doing next time you meet – but you do need to remember to follow up on that!

The start of the lesson should always be clear and, as much as possible, consistent so that a pattern is established in their minds. The model that you establish helps reassure them. It does away with the constant question, 'What are we doing today?', as they know they will be told, and the explanation will be given as soon as they are all in the room.

You will no doubt be given lots of procedures and expectations by your school regarding how they like the classroom to be for consistency. In all of this, I would encourage you to look for ways that the students themselves can become the regulators of their behaviour rather than yourself or the threat of punishment or sanctions. Seating plans and classroom layout again may get dictated by the school but if these are left to you, work with the class to establish the best working relationships for all. Also mention that at times you will change where people sit so as to mix up skill levels and make it easier for you to have one-to-ones with those who do find it harder to settle and focus. Putting them in the front near you will help, but also let them know that you are doing so in order that you can have easier chats with them to find a way to best help them focus and learn. It will provide you with quick 'get to know you' conversations to help establish the working relationship and find how best to make the lesson and learning meaningful for them.

The important thing to remember is that the students will be anxious and unsure about how you will be, and this will manifest itself in many silly often childish ways. Your confidence will help with the reassurance. The only person in the room you can directly control will be yourself, so make sure you always remember these are children looking for you to lead.

Reflection

At the end of term, or at other 'fresh start' times, use the space to reflect on what has gone well both academically as well as socially. Talk through what you liked about their progress, what impressed you in what they have done as a class and help them to recognise that you notice them as socially and emotionally capable people. Do your best to speak to everyone individually for just a few minutes, about what you have enjoyed about the time together, what you think of the journey you have both been on so far, and what steps you think they could take to try to improve over the next period. Reviews like this are often focused upon academic work, but I would always make the academic section a small part of the improvements they will need to do as they will already be aware of them through the lessons each week. Your time could and should be focused upon how they have grown and matured and the kind of adult that you are seeing develop in front of you. Set them personal targets but remember to ask their opinion of what you are saying and if they agree with your assessment. Make it personal and meaningful. The conversations may be for them strange at first as this will often be the first time they have had an adult speak to them in a reflective manner about their improvements in maturity. I am often told by students that I don't talk to them like other adults do, I talk to them *as* adults.

Challenge them to become the best they can be, and that means in other lessons as well as around school and their community.

These are just a few thoughts to take with you as you embark on the class. Please do smile right from the start and smile right to the end.

Chapter 5

Strategies for understanding and supporting primary school children

Primary school teachers have an amazing impact not only on how children learn to cope with education but also how they cope with the stress of having to learn new things which can often be outside of their own comfort zone and ability. It is vitally important as a primary school teacher to involve play, games and competitions to help embed the learning that is taking place. I often say, if you want a child to learn, play a game. If you want them to embed that learning, make it into a competition. Make the lessons fun and interactive. Use the outside as much as possible. Have them running around in the playground and use outdoor space as much as you can.

The brain is hard wired to play in a way that is often at conflict with the modern world. It wants to learn to climb, throw, run, chase, fight and make loud noises by shouting – all great skills to enable it to survive through life when hunting and being hunted were the normal environment that had to be faced and overcome every day. This often brings the child into conflict within the environment of school where all of those skills are frowned upon and discouraged and sadly punished, rather than expected and managed in a way that is appropriate for the young child who knows no different. Any of these elements can and should be used when trying to learn new academic things. Fighting is the one exception to the rule and this can be replaced by competitions.

As a primary school teacher, it is crucial that you bring some emotional stability to the child as soon as possible. From those first tentative steps that some take, to the realisation that making them go to school is not just a fad their parents are going through. I remember the story of one child asking his dad how long he would have to stay in school for, and the dad replied until you are eighteen. To which the child said, 'You will remember to come and get me, won't you?'

Building a sense of belonging and safety for the child right from the start is going to be key. Your kindness, warmth and patience are going to have to be constant every day. You will be awash in energy and excitement tinged with fear and uncertainty from them when they arrive, but you must be aware that your tone of voice and approach can be the difference between them wanting to come to school and learn or not.

They may have been influenced by their peers as to what to expect from school, as well as by their parents. The attitude of parents towards letting their child go on their own to the class once dropped off should be one of calm confidence. If you find that they are themselves anxious, your inspiring confidence is going to work for both them and their child. The child may well show anxiety, and this is normal and to be expected. Such anxiety is often forgotten about as they are welcomed by a smiling, caring teacher or support staff member eager to include them in activities which involve them being able to enjoy themselves and learn.

I always encourage primary school teachers to remember why they came into teaching. The reasons which are often given include to help, to teach and encourage children to be excited about learning. Try to make sure that your reasons are embedded into the very fabric of the class.

As the business of the year starts to unfold make sure that you revisit those words to see that they are still being given the priority they deserve. During primary school these words are extremely relevant to teaching the children social and emotional skills as much as the academic areas of learning. Belonging and emotional attachment must come first before any meaningful learning will take place.

Be very aware that at this age the influence of the teacher upon the class is very strong. By your actions you will be signalling to the children which of them is the one you most like and which is the one who is the naughtiest. This is often done unintentionally, but the consequences will be the same. I hear my grandchildren saying 'Naughty Peter got into trouble today'. I can guarantee that naughty Peter won't be invited to other people's houses to play. He may well have got the name because of his lack of social and emotional skills and these could and would improve with more positive interaction with others more skilled, yet his actions and the strategies that are used to correct his behaviour often make it harder for him to mix with other children as they see him as the one who disappoints the teacher. If a child needs correction then let the rest of the class as well as the child know how much they are still valued and liked. The actions are just a small part at this moment in their lives; they are learning how valued and important they are. Their emotions are very strong and vulnerable so treat them tenderly.

Rewards are often used to encourage children to stay on task and complete pieces of work and for some these form a good strategy for a short while. But remember that Peter will be left behind and again those positive strategies might actually be proving another area for him to fail in, and not be a part of the main class.

The introduction to brain maturation, contained within this book, highlighting some of the changes which will take place during the early years, should help you target most effectively your words and expectations. Tell the children what it is that you want. I just spoke to a primary teacher this week and they said they wanted children to listen, share and be polite. I asked them why and they were able to give me a good explanation. I then asked, have you explained the why to the children? So always explain the 'What it is you want' and then the 'Why they are going to be doing it'. This is vitally important regarding social and emotional development. This helps them understand and makes what they are doing more meaningful for them. Different levels of emotional and social skills need to be appreciated at these young ages. The children's own background, both social and economic, will often impact upon their ability to manage themselves. The children may have come from a home where they have never sat down and focused on an adult talking, or they may never have had to play in groups, or even understood the concept of sharing or taking turns. A lot of the social niceties of days gone by are lacking within some homes and this needs to be understood and managed. Your patience will be tested but will also be rewarded. As children get to know each other, remember it will often involve some of those hard-wired skills I mentioned before, such as running, chasing, shouting and wrestling. Try to see these for what they are and help turn them into positives by encouraging empathy and understanding and appreciation of alternative skills as well.

In Year 1 the children will enjoy the play and the opportunities to explore within the safe environment of school. In Year 2 I notice the children realising that school is a place of learning. You will have some who want to get back to the heady days of fun in Year 1 whilst others begin to enjoy the challenges of Year 2. I also notice during Year 2 those who show potential for learning and can indeed be stretched more than their peers. They may not want to sit with the others during circle mat time as they want to be more distinctive from the rest. Watch for the individuality of the students emerging and seek to engage them on a slightly more mature level than the rest. This is also a good age to spot those who might need more emotional and social intervention to prevent a larger problem when they are older.

One typical issue you will have during Year 2 is shoe laces. It may sound odd to focus on this, yet I have seen a number of teachers and support staff tying laces for children in Year 2 whilst others in the class have already mastered the skill, perhaps because of parents taking the time to teach it to them. If a Year 2 child seeks your help with laces, ask the whole class, 'Who has learnt the skill of tying laces?' Then when a sea of hands go up, ask, 'Who would like to come and help here?' I then let one child demonstrate their skill, to the class and you. It is a small step then for the skilled child to teach the other child during lunch or break if you don't think the parents will be able to have time. This is a great age for encouraging shared learning and experiences with each other. Make the most of it so it continues into the later years.

Years 2 and 3 are also a great time to listen to their personal understanding of the world and the things they have learnt. They are always keen to explain things to you and it's always rewarding to listen. A way to encourage them to form complete sentences whilst they explain things is to listen to their information first and then ask them to repeat it but this time don't say the word 'Errrrr', or whatever else they have a habit of including. To do this occasionally for them is a tough but fun challenge. Along with this you can play the 'yes/no' game with a bell. Ask a question, and then ask them to answer without saying either yes or no. It's simple but fun and has the bonus of helping you with aspects of the curriculum as well as they can be weaved into the sentence forming.

Children's time in primary school involves very many changes that their young bodies will go through. From the age of eight they will start to show signs of early adolescence and be looking for more adult input even though they are young. Be aware that through the year that you have them the target has to be their social and emotional advancement along with building their academic skills. They will reward you greatly as you help them develop a feeling of autonomy, and as they grow older before your very eyes.

You will have a lot of help and encouragement from your colleagues to help with the delivery of often very intense material for them. I would encourage you always to play to the children's strengths. At this age they are keen to learn, impress you and try new things. The more you make those things revolve around fun, encouragement and recognition the more fun and enjoyment you will all have. Start each year letting them know what is most important to you: kindness, friendliness, supporting one another, listening, helping, encouraging, enquiring, imagination, not giving up, trying, respect. Use those words to be the theme of the week for them, include everyone and help them to become champions in all of these skills. The world can never have enough kind people so within your class you can help create a few more. They will reward you by the way they tackle the academic items that underpin the reason you are there as well.

At the end of each year speak about the changes you have noticed in them regarding how they are maturing into caring socially able young people. Highlight to them the next step along their journey as they head towards the next year within the school. If you are able to have them reflect upon their biggest improvement and best memory then do so. Primary years see so many developments and it's important they are recognised with the children.

Chapter 6

Strategies for understanding and supporting teenagers through school

For those of you who are teaching in secondary schools you will be watching and contributing to the emergence of adults during their time with you. It will be challenging, frustrating, annoying, hard work, puzzling and in the end amazing – and that's just for the teenagers!

We, who have already gone through that stage, will now be on the receiving end of their emotions, questions, struggles, anxieties. And at the same time, we will be endeavouring to teach things which for them, as they deal with their everyday lives, will often seem irrelevant.

For some teenagers the transition will be fairly uneventful as they get on with their development both physically and emotionally without causing too many problems for themselves or those around them. For others this will not be the case, and the years that are meant to be helping them lay a platform for adulthood will in fact become very turbulent. We, who are working with them or caring for them hope they are going to come through it without having made too many bad choices which will have consequences in adulthood.

Your role in all this is to be consistent and help provide them with what they need emotionally and socially as well as academically to help them grow positively. As we have already seen, this means providing a BASE within your classroom. The more you are able to listen, share, challenge and encourage, the better it will be for them. They are looking for an alternative adult to act as a role model and mentor for them. Teachers as a whole need to recognise that they now play a far bigger role in the lives of teenagers than they have done in the past. For some the very act of going to school and meeting the same adults all the time is the most stable part of their lives. They spend on average six years of their lives under the influence of teachers within schools and this time can and should be used to help shape and influence them in the development of values and attitudes that will guide their later life. Hard work, curiosity, teamwork, communication and resilience are just a few of the skills that can and should be learnt in schools, along with empathy, tolerance and appreciation of others.

It is often thought by teachers that the role of talking to students, getting to know them and the issues they face should be confined to the students' mentors, support workers or school counsellors. They often say these people have more time and expertise to deal with the issues. The pressure to get through the curriculum, they argue, should take precedence over the pressing social and emotional needs of students within their classroom. This often leads to the students being excluded from the classroom as the classroom itself becomes the straw that broke the camel's back. I believe a significant improvement in the successful reintegration of students who have been excluded is the building of positive and supportive relationships with the teachers who have in the first place excluded them. All students have positive and rewarding conversations with those within the school who take the time to get to know them. This is often, for the most troubled students, confined to the support staff. You, as a teacher, can also have those constructive challenging conversations once you take the time. This will not only improve your own teaching skills and classroom relationships but provide you with far more understanding of the lives of those you wish to teach. I have never been in a school yet and found every teacher needing to use the behaviour policy in order to create a positive learning environment and have everyone engaged. There are always those who instead recognise that it is better to get to know the students, and form relationships with them, built upon clear expectations. Their reward for doing so is improved classroom behaviour and classroom atmosphere. Belonging comes before academic progress.

You can be that stable dependable adult that young people often need. For some of you, it might be sufficient just to be there for them for a specific part of their journey, or you may in fact be with them through all of it. You will recognise that every word you say positively or negatively could potentially take root in their minds and have an important impact.

The journey teenagers are travelling at this point in time is unlike any other in the history of the human race and their emotional and social mind is ill-equipped for all the fast paced, family and economic problems and insecurities the modern world now generates. The introduction of so many aspects of adult life to their young minds as well as the constant impact from social media is creating a very toxic environment for so many. The role models who in the past were there to stand as examples as to what is right and wrong are long gone. Gone also are the times when students could experiment just through play and imagination. Now they can experiment with all the things that are accessible to adults. Unfortunately, they still only have very immature brains when faced with all these adult scenarios and opportunities, ill-equipped to cope and often making poor choices.

As the teacher and adult in this ever-changing world, you need to keep things constant and consistent within your classroom, through your attitude and approach, enthusiasm and encouragement.

You are not there to control the students but to help them develop the skills needed to learn to control themselves. They are going through an amazing emotional and physical transition, searching for their own personal set of values and approaches to life. By your reaction to them and the situations you have to deal with, you will be showing and teaching them an attitude and approach that they could copy, so make sure yours is worth learning from and adopting.

Some teenagers may have had experiences that have made them wary of adults, having been let down by them in the past. This could present itself in their reaction to you. They might be pushing you away and being rude to you as they are protecting themselves from becoming close to an adult who they ultimately believe will again let them down. Some of the reasons for the behaviour you might experience will be outlined in the strategies section, later in the book. Slowly over time you will build up through your experiences possible causes and methods of helping but I hope this introduction will save you a lot of time and prevent you reacting in an emotional way with them. The part you play in your interaction should depend upon your own set of values and your appreciation of the important role you are now playing in their lives.

Teenagers will present different behaviours week by week and month by month because of the many changes in their brain. Therefore, always expect things to change rather than assuming because they behaved in a certain way one week, they will do it again next week. They are week older, a week more mature and their brain has developed a bit more. You will see the changes over six months and especially over the years within your classroom so adapt as appropriate and always try to stay a step ahead by using the charts I have provided regarding brain maturation (pp. 14–20).

They will ask you many questions, and you should be prepared to ask them lots of questions as well about what they think, feel, understand and what their values and aspirations are. You will be delighted with the results the more you ask them. To start they may not be able to provide you with many answers but the more you encourage them to think the more they will provide you with their thoughts. It is truly an amazing time and one that should be seen for what it is: a transition from childhood into adulthood as they shake off their childishness and seek their own life.

Link as much as you can from your specialist subject into their lives. The more you keep it relevant and meaningful the better. Remember also that they are only really interested in the here and now up until around the age of 15. So, stay away from telling them about what the topic will be good for in their adult life as they only want to know why they are learning this thing now! Once they have reached the age of 15 they start to explore more possibilities regarding their own future and the realisation that they will soon be leaving school. It has more to do with their brain accessing the last part of its maturation (the neocortex) than it does with the fact that they only have a couple of years of school left.

Start as you mean to go on and the more you talk to them about the maturity you will see from their attitude and approach to issues the more they will respond, as seeking to become more mature is part of their own quest. Emotions are very strong and peer pressure is at its maximum around the age of 14, so be aware that they think more of what their friends and those around them think of them than you do. Be aware that at that age they will always want to save face so being strong, rude and sarcastic to you may be one way they keep in with their friends. So, if these things happen, remember to talk to them about how inappropriate such behaviour is when you have some time alone with them. At the time you can say, 'You and I will have a talk about what you just said and I need to see you at ….' They often think after the event and obviously we are looking to master the skills of thinking before they speak. So, you can say to them, 'I want you to just think about what you just said, and I will ask you again and expect a different response.'

Be prepared to share some things about yourself when asked but be aware of what is and is not appropriate. Some of the questions can become too personal and you can let them know the areas you are willing to discuss with them and those that are not appropriate.

Use the term maturity a lot when explaining about the expectations you have for them within the classroom. Especially through secondary school, students dislike being treated as children even though the behaviour they demonstrate is childish. The expectations you set them at the start of each term should reflect the improvements in emotional and social maturity that you are wanting to see from them. This can also become the starting point of conversations with them as they can explain what areas of maturity they find harder to demonstrate. Discuss with them aspects of maturity they like and which they think they could improve upon. None of these conversations take a great deal of time and will reap dividends in the future as they work maturely with each other and the work that has been set them.

Discuss the qualities that you like within your classroom and again ask for opinions from them about your selection. They will value the time spent having 'mature conversations' with you. Link those qualities to the work environment as well as the classroom and share with them the idea that the classroom is like a working environment and that the more they get on and cooperate the better the quality of life is for them all.

No two classrooms are going to be the same, as the individuals within will play a large part in creating the environment. Your role will be to mould the classroom towards your own preferred working environment, which we will discuss in the next section.

Sleep and diet also play an important role during this time as students now have more control over both and don't always make the best choices. Recently I was speaking to a 14-year-old girl who was constantly out of lessons, getting into trouble. I asked about her diet and she explained to me that she never eats breakfast but has a bar of chocolate at break, and then she may have chocolate spread for tea. She also likes flavoured crisps which she has in the evening as well. She doesn't eat dinner at home as her mum doesn't always cook. She was able to explain to me that she knows it's wrong but, in her mind, she was managing. I explained to her that her body was letting her know as best it could that it wasn't coping. I asked, 'Are you tired most of the time?' 'Do you find it hard to concentrate?' 'Do you argue with your friends and family?' She answered yes to all these things and we quickly looked at how different calories are either good or bad for you and how she was probably starving her body of all things it needs at that moment.

The most important thing was me just asking questions and making statements as to what she said to show I was listening. I was just curious as to why she chose not to look after herself. She said she would from that point on, and I asked, 'Why?', in a curious tone. And then she explained to me that she wanted to change and also what she was going to do differently. All I said at the end was that it sounded like a good plan. The tone at this point was matter of fact. I needed her to try to convince me of her changed attitude. The entire conversation took place over five minutes. At lunch time she came to find me to show me what sandwich she had bought. I said I was looking forward to hearing how she is coping when her body is on better form. We were both smiling at this point. When dealing with students during secondary school bear in mind how much lack of sleep and lack of food will be impacting upon their own ability to cope. You will see this referred to time and again as you search for reasons as to why someone does what they do. At all costs avoid telling them what they should do or what would be good for them. Nine times out of ten they already know that. You are the adult, and it's your role to help them unlock the problem and then help them to come up with a solution themselves. That is a skill they can use for the rest of their lives.

At this age, patronising attitudes from adults are highly felt and must be avoided at all costs. I ask teachers if their your family or partners ever say to them, 'Don't use that teacher tone with me!' If they know their family doesn't like it, why persist with it with students at school? They also don't like it! Get rid of the teacher tone. Imagine you have a group of adults in front of you and speak with the same tone. The words and explanation may need to change due to their levels of understanding, but the tone should be the same.

Generation Z wants more frequent communication than the Millennials to help them stay engaged and on track (The Center for Generational Kinetics, 2018).

I believe this constant reassurance and positive feedback is led by the constant interaction within social media and the need for acceptance. This need for constant feedback provides you with a tremendous opportunity to develop their mindset, attitude and focus. Simple two-minute conversations can benefit both you and your students, saving you significant time in the future.

These are just a few points to consider in your dealing with students through the secondary school years. They change from their childish remnants of primary school and early adolescence through the challenging period of adolescence as they search for their personal identity, finally emerging as a young adult. Challenge them with high expectations and encourage them to become the best they can be for themselves.

References

The Center for Generational Kinetics. (2018) *The State of Generation Z*. Austin, TX: The Center for Generational Kinetics. Available at: https://genhq.com/annual-gen-z-research-study/ (accessed 17 December 2019).

Chapter 7

Strategies for supporting students with SEND

Sonia Allen

Over the length of time you will be teaching not only will you be experiencing many emotional and social issues within your classroom, but you will also become familiar with the various special educational needs and disabilities (SEND) of the children and students you teach. They sometimes will have an Educational Health Care Plan (EHCP) outlining for you various things to take into account when teaching them, including their needs and strategies to help with differentiation. The most common SEND you will encounter are attention deficit hyperactivity disorder (ADHD), autism and dyslexia.

The aim for you as a teacher will be to familiarise yourself as much as possible with the differences/difficulties children or students with a diagnosis present, to recognise the signs as a possible reason why they may be struggling (if you have not been informed beforehand), and to prepare not only your lessons but the whole environment to take into account these needs. Diagnoses of autism and ADHD in children are steadily rising for a variety of reasons, therefore your skill set needs to be ready to offer the best for those children so as to make their schooling successful and increase their confidence and self-esteem.

The strategies below are for your information, to share with your TA, along with the support of the SENDCO. The more you are able to meet the needs of every SEND child you encounter, the more your skill as a teacher will improve for the rest of the class. It will also help reduce incidents of disturbance caused by a child or students with SEND, as their needs are now being met.

Students with attention deficit hyperactivity disorder

In the past, attention deficit hyperactivity disorder (ADHD) was considered to be a condition which children had but would 'grow out of'. However, we now know that it is a neurological condition which spans a lifetime, often with added specific learning difficulties such as dyslexia, dyspraxia, dyscalculia and behavioural disorders.

ADHD is characterised by impulsive and hyperactive behaviours, as well as distractibility and inattention, thought to be caused by a chemical imbalance in the brain.

You will be very aware of children or young people with this condition as they struggle to sit still, to keep their attention focused and to maintain their self-control. They may seem to day-dream and can be absent minded and forgetful. Without meaning to (*this is important to remember*) they often act in ways which really disrupt the class. You may find that during social times, they often play happily with children or have friends some two years younger than themselves.

Again, it is really important for you to liaise with your SENDCO for background information, and to talk with parents, so the children or young people understand you are all in contact. Remember to contact parents with some good news regularly as well as when the student may be struggling to settle – this will show the parents you recognise how much it takes for this student to conform to class/social boundaries.

There are sometimes issues, around the start of Year 9 in secondary schools, especially with boys who are on medication for ADHD. This is often due to the fact they tend to have a growth spurt around then and the medicine they are taking may need to be increased, so ask the SENDCO to check with parents if you notice an increase in disruptive behaviours.

However, using the key strategies outlined below will help the individual, you and your class to work together and support each other through a better understanding of what works.

- Place the student near you with their back to the rest of the class – avoid distraction areas/stimuli such as windows as this will help them to focus on just you, not what others are doing behind. Have good role models near them to encourage peer learning.
- Ensure they understand what the objective of their work is; ask them to explain what they have to do back to you to avoid confusion and misinterpretation.
- Allow some flexibility of down time during long periods of learning, where they will struggle. Have an area they know they can go, to find something they enjoy doing for a mini break.
- Allow use of manipulation objects when sitting, such as tangles or, if older, a doodle book, as long as you are sure they can still focus. Consider the use of headsets to reduce distractions.
- Allow controlled movement around the room. This can be built upon by sending them on an 'errand' say to the class next door if they need two minutes out of the class (arrange with a colleague that if this student turns up, just to give them a book/worksheet etc).
- Try to avoid changes as this will negatively stimulate the student. If changes are necessary, make sure the student is aware of this as far in advance as possible and monitor closely on any school trips. Areas such as canteens, drama halls etc will be challenging for students with ADHD to manage due to the acoustics, so ensure there is support and understanding from these colleagues too. You can easily share good practice of what has worked in your class and some de-escalation techniques they can use.
- Most importantly, build a good relationship together and remember to reward and give effective praise for the times when they get it right.

Students and children with autism/autism spectrum condition

Autism spectrum condition (ASC) is an umbrella term to describe people who have a common set of characteristics related to their ability to communicate in a social world.

ASC is a neuro-developmental disorder that impacts on normal brain development.

Students with autism may often struggle with managing their behaviour, and there is always a reason behind this – usually because they are anxious or having difficulties and so will go into their 'defence mode'. Try to think of these 'behaviours' as anxiety attacks rather than that they are just being naughty.

Put yourself in the shoes of a student with ASC. Often they have fears of everyday things we cannot relate to, so imagine being scared of:

- The colour orange – how many orange objects are there on the way to school and throughout their day!
- Lightning/storms/heavy rain – I have had to calm many a student with ASC during stormy days in school.
- Being touched by other people – this affects almost all students with the condition, so be very aware of this when supporting them through any anxiety attacks. Although with younger children, I have found that standing behind them and firmly stroking down their arms helps to calm them quickly.
- Conversation – as they grow, they do realise that 'normal' conversation is tricky for them so give plenty of warning if you want them to speak out in class or answer questions.
- Interaction with other people – a lot of anxiety arises when they start a new year/class/ group as it takes a long time to get used to new people. Try to set them up with someone they are familiar with in these situations.

There are many ways as their teacher you can support them to minimise these anxieties. The following strategies will help and assist many students in your class, not just those with diagnosed SEND:

Communication

- Students or young children with ASC are easily overloaded with information, so it is always easier for them to process information if given step by step. Visual supports such as pictures and the use of bullet points to spread out instructions and at each stage will help them process their thoughts easier and explain their needs and wants clearly. This will also help you to see what work they can manage and where they need to be stretched.
- Call their name before you ask a question, reduce your language and if necessary, give extra thinking time once you've asked it, for example, saying you will come back to them for their answer if they struggle.
- Also remember, instructions may be taken very literally, so ensure you are clear and unambiguous. Sayings we use every day without realising can make no sense whatsoever to students, a young person, with ASC, e.g. 'Pull your socks up/please take a seat/put those books down'.
- Students with ASC often cannot understand others not following the rules and have their own distinct interpretation of what is fair and unfair. If there is a rule (especially unwritten social rules) they are struggling with, draw up a written list of what is accepted and what isn't, especially as this can vary from class to class as well as year on year. This will then come in handy for the whole class to adhere to. Be prepared to change this as they come across new social situations and need help to comprehend.

Visual support

- Prepare well ahead for any change – whether change of room/teacher/activity.
- Using a visual timetable stuck in an easy to see place will reassure and support with consistency. Often a 'trigger' for anxiety is an unexpected, sudden change of plan.
- If students and young children are taught how to recognise their own behaviour triggers, they can learn to be proactive in helping themselves before the situation becomes critical. Try using visual 'anger thermometers', which show how they feel physically on one side and what positive things they can do to calm on the other. Support them in drawing whatever happens to them, butterflies in tummy, screwing up face, headaches, etc.
- If the student is experiencing negative thoughts (self-doubt), support them in writing these thoughts down, then vigorously screw up the paper and bin it. The student and young person often feel they have then 'got rid of' these thoughts to make way for a more positive outlook. Go through these drawings with them to help them understand that at any stage, there are ways of dealing with their anger/anxiety and for them to be able to recognise these stages for themselves.
- Another good use of visuals is storyboard conversations. These are useful for going through cause and effect with students, you don't have to be an artist, in fact the simpler the drawing the better – draw stick people but make sure you draw in the emotions as this is what the student with ASC struggles to understand.

  For example, if they have lashed out at another person – draw one stick person kicking/smacking/punching with an angry face, then show the other as very upset in the face. Explain why this behaviour is against the rules, how the other students feel and what can be done to stop this in future. If you date and log these storyboards, often a pattern of behaviour can be seen as to when trigger points/times are likely to occur. This may be social times such as break, lunch and between lessons when class rules are not so adhered to.

Strategies for unstructured times

Many students with ASC really struggle at unstructured times during the school day, due to misunderstanding of social communications.

Wherever possible it is always in the student's best interest to mix with their peers as much as possible but for times when they need to be alone, you can use resources like a pop-up tent in the corner of the room or a quiet area they can be calm in. If you are lucky enough you may be able to create a sensory room. I have seen this done in an old stock cupboard to great effect, and with minimal funds. Even a table against a wall in a quieter area of the class with their favourite activity will help.

- Try to always have at least half a wall completely clear of pictures/posters/writing – this will create a calming effect if they can be sat in front of it.
- On this note, after a holiday or even a weekend, stand on the threshold of your classroom and take a really long look at it; most are far too cluttered with colour and pictures and information and students' work and resources from floor to ceiling, sometimes even over windows and doors. What can you do to create a clear, uncluttered area for your students and young children, with SEND?
- Headphones are a great comfort for times like rainy breaks when the levels of noise in the rooms is higher than normal and for high acoustic rooms such as canteens or drama rooms.

- Their own special interest can be used as reward time, just be careful to set an agreed time. Try to limit this, as it can be difficult to drag them away from once they get engrossed. Another tip is to use a large timer for this as a visual, so it will not be you verbally telling them to stop all the time.
- Use of a stress vest for younger children may help with relaxation; they enjoy the feeling of being supported firmly, whilst not actually being touched, which many do not like. A weighted lap mat does the same job and can be easily made if funds are not available.
- Obviously, it is very important that you build good relationships with your students, and especially so with those who have SEND. They will grow to trust your judgement if they learn that you are fair and, above all, consistent in your approach. They will have difficulty showing how much they rely on your support, but you will gradually come to understand their behaviours, and this will be a reflection of how they are feeling – you will certainly know immediately when they are anxious or scared of something!
- Liaise with your SENDCO regularly to get all the background information you can on students with SEND, especially after any professional or parental meetings. The more you know about them, the more you can relate to how they act and achieve at school. Similarly, if you are using a strategy which works and gets the best out of them, share this good practice with other colleagues. For example, knowing what their favourite subject is, whether school based or a hobby, is a good diffuser to talk about if they have had an anxiety attack or are feeling especially vulnerable.
- Often even getting to school has already increased their stress levels just by perhaps running out of their favourite breakfast, or the bus was a little late, or they couldn't find their book …. It will not take much on top of this to tip them over the edge at school. To counter this very real possibility, meet and greet them to gauge how they are feeling. Set the agenda for the day, discuss something positive with them they can focus on and hopefully you can avert a crisis later in the day. I often speak to teachers who have had to deal with a meltdown, and they say, 'Well he came into school with a mood on to begin with … '. This can so easily be averted with just a friendly greeting and a question such as 'How was your morning so far?' If you are lucky enough to have a TA, this could be one of their morning routines to help settle these vulnerable students.
- Finally, another strategy I've used to encourage a deeper understanding and support from others is to chat with the student's class, explaining what autism is and how they can help to support their classmate. This needs to be arranged through the SENDCO, with parental involvement and the permission of the student, who can be there or not depending on what they feel more comfortable with. It helps to explain to the other students why he/she is having issues, how they can help and (importantly) what their strengths are. Good resources for this are: Rosie King's TED Talk, 'How autism freed me to be me' (https://youtu.be/jQ95xlZeHo8); *The Curious Incident of the Dog in the Night-time*, by Mark Haddon; *I'm Not Strange, I Have Autism: Living with an Autism Spectrum Disorder*, by Ellen Van Gelder.

Students with dyslexia

Dyslexia usually arises from a weakness in the processing of language-based information. Biological in origin, it tends to run in families, but environmental factors also contribute. Dyslexia can occur at any level of intellectual ability. Dyslexia causes difficulties in learning to read, write and spell. Short-term memory, mathematics, concentration, personal organisation may also be affected.

Whichever resources you put in place for those students with either diagnosed dyslexia or dyslexic tendencies, or even those who struggle to read, once they are set up, they will be there for you to use year in year out and to share as good practice with other colleagues, so it is well worth the initial couple of hours getting them together.

In every school I have supported, I've suggested they buy in extra SEND resources, a pack for each class, which works out at about £15 at the time of writing. They contain useful items which lots of students find helpful, not just those with SEND, resources such as:

Reading rulers – used a lot when reading from textbooks, as they minimise the glare of black writing on white paper and break up the text into either small paragraphs or into single lines, depending on how the student likes to read.

Timers – use to set small, timed targets, e.g. one minute to get the date and title written down, two minutes to start a new paragraph (using laminated sentence starters to support), three minutes to think of your start, middle and end etc. Timers also reduce the need for frequent verbal reminders to continue/start work.

Coloured overlays (in packs of several colours) – these can be cut in half from A4 to A5 to spread the cost and often help students to 'fix' the words on the page and to cut black and white glare. Sometimes the student needs to try a couple of colours until they find the one which suits their eyesight best, and often I've seen adults use them, especially in the afternoon when eyes are tired.

Pen grips – often a surprisingly useful resource and not just for primary schools in helping younger children to hold the pen correctly and form their letters properly. Students in secondary schools have said they provide support to their fingers when having to write lots of work at once.

Twister tangles – these are a SENDCO's/teacher's best friend! A loop of twisty soft plastic which can be given to those students who need to fidget, this is really useful as it focuses their attention and it is *silent* to use! Lay down some basic rules before it is given, to ensure it will not be taken apart or given to anyone else, and that it is to be used either in their jacket pocket or on their lap so as not to distract others. A tip to spread the budget is to take two tangles and break them up to make three smaller ones.

Think about your printed materials – An easy win is to use a larger font for all print outs. Also, use pastel coloured paper with a dark blue text as this reduces eye strain which black text on white paper can produce. Sans serif fonts – such as Arial and Comic sans – are popular as the letters can appear less crowded.

Split text with bullet points and use bigger line spacing. Break up text with visuals and prompts. All of this will support and aid any student who has difficulty reading and making sense of the text in front of them.

Think about 'labels' – for those dyslexic students who may lose their 'mojo', remind them that they have a learning 'difference' not a learning difficulty. Their brain just learns in a different way and often this difference produces highly creative people, imaginative artists and successful business entrepreneurs such as Albert Einstein, Leonardo da Vinci and more recently Walt Disney, Richard Branson and Tom Cruise, to name a few famous dyslexics.

Differentiation: How to (easily) help your students achieve their potential

When I discuss differentiation with teachers, often their response is 'Yes, I would love to have all this differentiated work for my students, but I just don't have time!'

My response is that you will gain time back many times over if the work you set your students is meaningful to them, they feel they can achieve it and are confident in attempting it independently. As part of your Quality First Teaching, this should be an integral part of your planning and you will derive a lot of satisfaction from seeing how easily your different ability students achieve their potential.

Try not to reinvent the wheel though, check with colleagues first if they have any previous work they have set for your year group/individuals, and also remember to ask all TAs who have worked with them as they often have wonderful materials prepared for students they know well. Then be prepared to share the resources you build up with others too. A NQT will always remember a colleague who has shared and supported them in their frantic first few months of teaching.

With the World Wide Web at our fingertips, it has never been easier to look up information and there are literally hundreds of ways to differentiate. Whenever I have delivered training on this to staff, it has always opened up discussion amongst them on who has what materials and open sharing of good practice, often because others are simply not aware that you are looking for ideas.

The following strategies are the ones I have found most useful, in that I have been able to see students so pleased with themselves and their work (done mostly independently), simply because they could understand the information put in front of them.

- Work sheets – There is nothing worse for a student struggling to achieve than to be given a sheet of paper with a full page of solid text on it. I have watched some students' whole body language seem to deflate as they then look around at others getting on with the work. This is where they often decide to cause a distraction rather than admit they cannot access the work in front of them. Create a series of work sheets which increase in difficulty, for your students to decide which to access. These can be colour coded too. For the high achievers, have open questions or tasks. Break up blocks of text with highlighted key words/main points, use visuals, a larger size font and prompts for sub headings etc. Reduce the language you use and the amount of sentences they have to write up. Give plenty of examples.

- Traffic light objectives – Highlight what you expect ALL the class to achieve, MOST to get to and SOME to achieve. Once you have set the objective, give your class a couple of minutes to discuss with each other what they have to do, as this quickly establishes who has understood it and who has not. You could create BUZZ groups for this too: ask students to discuss in pairs what they have to do. They will feel more confident speaking to each other than to a whole class looking at them. The sound of ten or so pairs of children chatting about the objective or next steps is a good way to energise the class and get started. Mostly, teachers address work to the 'middle' groups, often because it's the safest point for most students to 'get' it. However, try to make a conscious effort within the lesson to aim to the higher or lower achievers. Set the tone with 'I'm sure you are all aware of this but just to remind everyone', or 'This may sound difficult but let me go through it with you.'

- Keywords and definitions – Set up a board for the keywords of the week or term, giving their definitions. This will be an easy reference point for all students, not just those who have difficulty retaining the information. You could appoint a new 'word monitor' each week to observe any new words in work, especially for new topics. Before using new keywords, set pairs off to see who knows the definition of the word. A dictionary 'champion' can also be appointed weekly, whose job it is to look up the definition of new words and feed back to the class.

- Peer helpers – As the more able students finish tasks, they can move around to support those who need more help, and take their work with them to show as a visual. (Ensure the more confident ones do not do the work for others, they are just there to advise!) Or you can create an Expert corner: those who complete the work can move to a separate place and those who wish to can go to them for advice.
- Options – Open activities – Students have different ways they enjoy learning. Set a couple of questions they must answer with an open agenda for learning, the only rule being that they show evidence of their work to you. Set examples, such as making a poster of the answers, or writing a poem, making a drawing, or producing a small set piece of drama – however they feel they are best at putting information together.
- Challenger work – For your high achievers (often some students with SEND) always have an extension task ready, you can even challenge them further by having different levels of extensions (RAG them). These can be printed off to be kept at a certain point where the student can access them independently. Often students will become distracted if they nothing to further challenge their thinking.
- Wonder wall – Often students ask the most amazing questions but there is often not time to go into the answers in any detail. Create a wonder wall for when a good question is asked, get them to write it on a post it and stick it on the wall. When students have finished their work, they can take a question and research/explore it either independently or with a partner. They could then feed their findings back to the class.
- Student presentations – Divide the class into groups to research together and deliver their findings to the rest of the class as a presentation. Set some examples to prevent 'boring' presentations, e.g. ask them to make a handout (no reading from slides!), or develop a set piece of drama, invent a game, or create an interactive discussion piece. Ask the groups to JUSTIFY their claims, which they can all do, just some at more advanced levels than others. This will encourage their reasoning skills.
- Effective questions – As well as asking your lower level thinking questions, e.g. 'What can you tell me about that?', 'Can you give me an example?', 'How do you compare it to … ?' Also establish a routine of asking higher-level thinking questions, especially for your high achievers, which can help create extension tasks, e.g. questions based on drawing connections, justifying ideas, investigating new concepts. These will include thinking out of the box questions (scenarios, ideologies) and exam style questions. Also, establish a routine where there is a no hands up question time so you can ask those who often don't get a chance to answer – this will give you an opportunity to ask questions to embed the learning, follow through on any misconceptions, and encourage their thinking/reasoning skills.
- Thinking time – Always allow this for your lower ability and SEND students. For younger ones you can set a timer (30 seconds/1 minute). Ask your question, then say you will come back to them, which gives them time to process the information they need to come up with an answer and will give them confidence to want to answer further questions.

Effective use of teaching assistants

If you are lucky enough to have a teaching assistant (TA) working with you then you will undoubtedly want to have the best working relationship possible to ensure the smooth efficiency of your classroom environment and student progress. Try to think of them as your para-professional and use them as such. The best working practice I ever saw was in observing a class for a good five minutes before I established which was the teacher and who was the TA – this was also an outstanding lesson, funnily enough!

Make time to get to know your TA – what is their skillset, their interests, their hobbies? The more you know about them, the more you can incorporate their skills into your students' life experiences. Which other years or students have they worked with? Are they running any interventions out of class? Do they have useful resources and student information they can share with you? In secondary school, you as the teacher may only see this student for English or Science or whatever subject you teach, whereas often the TA follows them through the curriculum, so may have very relevant knowledge of strategies which work with a certain individual. Don't be afraid to ask 'What works for them in other lessons?' and 'Have you noticed anything they struggled with?'

TAs have lots of information regarding the needs of SEND students from regular liaison with the SENDCO, SEND training events and from delivering various interventions, so ask them to feed back to you anything relevant to help support and build relationships with SEND students you teach.

Unfortunately, I have spoken with teachers who were even unsure of their TA's name, which was a very sorry state of affairs for both of them. If you are working in a larger Academy school, have a discussion with your TA around their timetable to establish exactly when you are likely to have their support so you can plan together. Your TA will be very effective support only if they are clear on your Learning Objectives and Outcomes for your lesson. (Discuss with them how the work you are setting builds on previous learning, and where the learning will go next.) Also, in some schools, realistically there is little time for feedback regarding student progress at the end of a lesson, so try to build in just a few minutes while the students are on task or checking their work to ask how the student has done or listen to your TA explain how they feel the lesson has gone with certain individuals.

So, lets imagine you have a TA regularly, the same one. It is important your students see you both as equal adults to help to build respect, therefore when you deliver your objective or start a new topic make sure the TA is standing at the front with you. They can be writing keywords up, holding the text book open at the correct page, showing the different resources available to use, or any similar modelling to show the class that they are on board with the planning, delivery and support of everybody in this lesson with you.

Remember though that your TA is not your differentiation and neither are they there to constantly support the lower ability, SEND groups or consistently manage those who struggle with behaviour. Students of all abilities should consistently work with both the teacher and the TA to ensure the quality of teaching and time spent with them by both adults.

A good strategy to ensure this happens is 'Rotating Tables': for example, if you have five tables in your class, the two adults move from table to table independently offering support; in between, students will be working independently, then together on collaborative group work, then with peer support for checking of work. This strategy covers all areas of student working.

Ask your TA to deliver your starter or plenary sometimes; this will give you an opportunity to catch up with those who need some pre or post learning and you get a whole new outlook on your class if now and then you stand at the back observing your class while the TA is at the front.

Your TA will also have a bank of SEND resources, as mentioned earlier, available to the SEND team which can prove very effective in class. These include reading rulers, coloured overlays, tangles, timers, pencil grips etc. Find out what they have and try these out with students who struggle. Do try several times, as it takes a few attempts with some students for them to realise how effective these resources can be for them.

Above all, build up a relationship with your TA to enable you both to experience a really effective working practice together.

Chapter 8

Strategies for de-escalation, distraction and diversion

One of the greatest skills you will acquire throughout your teaching career will be the use of techniques that help you to calm situations you see in front of you when behaviour starts to become an issue.

These de-escalation techniques are used to defuse situations, caused by a variety of reasons, some of which you may well be unaware of. Or it may be the better course of action simply because to confront the issue head on will in fact either make the matter worse or disrupt the lesson and spoil relationships.

It means we, as the adults in the room, need to be the ones using our emotional intelligence, as the trigger that starts the incident will also be triggering our emotions as well. Remember that when a situation arises outside of what is expected, especially if it goes against what we are wanting to happen, our brain starts to use the subcortex, triggering our amygdala and so preparing us for an emotional response.

Unpicking a scenario

I was talking with a Year 6 teacher recently, and he told me of an incident that had happened earlier that week. He explained he was telling the extra students arriving in his class, which was already full of his own class, that they had no chairs left to sit on and they needed to find somewhere to sit on the carpet. One student, who was already sitting down said, 'You can't tell me where to sit.'

The teacher pointed out to him that he was already sitting down, and in any case, he wasn't addressing him directly. The boy then, under his breath, called him a 'crackhead'. (This is a clear trigger for the teacher.) The teacher then told me, 'I felt he was probably thinking that I hadn't heard what he said, so I said', 'Sorry, I didn't hear that, can you tell me again what you just said?' The boy said, 'Nothing.' The teacher (even more triggered) then said, 'I distinctly heard you say something. What was it?' To which the boy then said, for everyone to hear, 'Crackhead.' The teacher then asked him to step outside, which the boy refused to do. So, leadership was called, and the boy was removed. The teacher, when explaining this to me, was looking for confirmation from me that the boy should have been suspended and not in school the next day. He felt that, as no stern punishment had been issued, the boy would think he has the right to go calling the teacher names in the future, and that he would again get away with it!

The question I was asked was, 'What do you think?'

Before I answered we spent a little time looking at the whole incident. So, let's unpick what has gone on.

To begin with, the number of children in his class was exceptional. He was temporarily looking after extra children as they had just returned from a trip at the end of the day. Let's be aware that anything that changes the norm causes some to be more unsettled than usual.

For those whose classroom it was, namely the boy who made the comment, the others were coming into his room, so he seems to feel at that particular moment he needed to express himself. (In his mind, his Model is out of sync.)

The teacher then *told* them what to do: 'Sit on the carpet as there are no more chairs.'

> *10 to 11-year-olds, already in early adolescence, are beginning to clash with authority. Some don't like being told what to do as they feel they lose control and give power to others when they follow their orders.*

The boy used this command from the teacher to make himself known to others, highlighting the fact he doesn't take orders, even though he was not directly being spoken to.

> *Recognise the instructions you give are also having an impact and might look like a judgement on those within earshot, even though they are not directly affected by the instructions. Your audience is always everyone who hears you. There is never a time when your words and actions are not being evaluated by others and put into the prism of their understanding. You can in fact be creating memories that they associate with feelings that are only raised again when they see you once more, and that could be weeks or months and in some cases years after the event that took place. The memories you create need to be positive. Your shouting on the playground, especially if it scared someone, may be the first impression a person has of you and will be remembered when the students or child enters your classroom and properly meets you for the first time in the future.*

When you hear a child or student give a verdict or make a statement regarding what you are doing, check to see if it is in conflict or agreement, as this is your cue for understanding their viewpoint and state of emotion. For the student in the scenario, in saying those words he highlighted his feelings toward authority and his relationship with the teacher.

The teacher focused on the statement and answered it factually.

This was the point in which the student's anxiety became even more heightened as he now had to engage with the person whom, as he has just pointed out, can't tell him what to do. The student was now being forced into talking to the authority figure.

Instead of engaging, he decided the thing to do was verbalise his annoyance by calling the teacher a name, only just loud enough for a limited audience to hear.

This is enough for the teacher to be triggered, and therefore to need to address this rudeness and lack of respect. The teacher thus shifts into fight mode to regain authority. All of this is very reasonable and understandable if we are dealing with people being reasonable and understanding. Unfortunately, in this case reason and understanding had left the room, to be replaced by emotion.

The boy was now being pushed into having to say the word again, but this time, the whole class could hear. This raised the incident to a different level, which required the teacher to feel he should defend his position even more and demand that the student must leave the room.

The boy had already stated that no one can tell him what to do. So now unfortunately, he was having to stand by that statement he made, as he was now being told what to do by the teacher – the very thing he had already highlighted was an issue to him in the first place. He had nowhere to go at this point, and would therefore, in this circumstance, rather be told off than lose face and credibility. Therefore, he stood his ground.

Senior leadership was called, and the boy left. The boy's argument wasn't with the senior leaders – he had proved his point to the rest of the class and the teacher. He had made his point and raised his profile. All of which was very negative and unfortunate for him.

When I explained this interpretation and explanation of events to the teacher, he had already recognised he himself had been triggered when he thought about it later in the day. For some people, once you've started down this path it's hard to back track.

We then looked at alternative courses of action as well as how to talk to the boy in question, later in the day, so as to rebuild a relationship necessary for the boy to be able to learn educationally as well as socially. He agreed that together they could both look at alternative strategies for when things don't go to plan.

So, what was the alternative?

Hopefully you will recognise that the start of the incident wasn't when the child made the comment, it was from when the classroom was becoming crowded with new people arriving. The change in the norm affects their sense of coherence (Model), so you need to be prepared for any alterations affecting those you are responsible for. These changes may have a negative impact or raise anxiety within those it has affected, and they may act out of character by being silly as well as making negative silly comments.

The comment or command by the teacher to bring order to the situation is understandable, yet, when talking with children, especially those over the age of 7, it is important to provide them with the opportunity to maintain some sense of autonomy within their lives. So, try to provide them with choices when wanting them to do something.

We looked therefore at alternative ways to explain to those entering the room what they could now do as all the seats have been taken. We agreed that we could have said,

> As you can see all the seats have been taken so you need to find yourself a place that doesn't disturb those already seated. We have room on the mat or you can stand around the room as it will only be for a few minutes.

In this way you are providing them with the choice they need to maintain their sense of autonomy. You can also see those who can act more responsibly as well.

In light of these two things, the response to the direct command and the arrival of new people, was for the boy to make a comment. 'No one tells me where to sit.' At this stage it wasn't directed at anyone in particular it was just stating a fact of how he feels. We can assume from what he was saying that he was not in a very happy place.

> *When you do get comments from people, look for the motivation as well as the message – look for the inference behind the facts that are being stated.*

As the conversation progressed and the facts were stated by the teacher as to what he was doing, and therefore had nothing to do with him, it built up to a negative comment aimed at the teacher.

I am sad to say that negative statements towards teachers are commonplace and you will have to be prepared in dealing with children and students going through a range of emotional situations that at times it will spill out towards those nearest to them. Do your best to be prepared for this to happen and when, unfortunately, it does, always start by examining what has led up to the situation, to start to understand the reason and find the best solution. Remain patient and emotionally intelligent. Your calmness will help.

If someone does make a comment you deem to be out of order, and especially when it shows disrespect, you do need to address it. Imagine it's like them hitting the ball into your court. You play the ball back when you are good and ready, and it may be that you decide to do so later. So, to let them know you will address the comment just simply say, 'Ryan, I hear what you are saying, and you and I will have a chat later.' In this way the whole class knows it will be addressed and you can maintain your leadership of the situation. It also gives you time to think about what led up to them hitting the ball over to you in the first place. If we carry on with the tennis analogy, as in a tennis game, the way the person is hitting their shot to you should have a lot to do with how you return it. If you just bash it back, without first understanding the spin, the swerve, or the speed, you are no longer in control, it could go anywhere. Just as can happen in your conversation. If your mind can process all these scenarios quickly on a tennis court, then so your mind will get used to processing the many factors associated with a comment within a classroom.

Remember, the importance of your role is to always recognise you are a teacher and sometimes you have to become a teacher of manners and emotions as well. The only way this will be effective is if you maintain your relationship with the one you are trying to teach.

As mentioned, in this circumstance, the teacher needed to talk with the boy, as the situation does need to be addressed. They both can learn from each other through this experience, and therefore turn what was a negative experience for both of them back into a positive one.

I highlighted to the teacher that it is also important to look for alternatives to their actions so that both can in the future prevent issues arising again. The aim of the next conversation was to build relationships. The teacher is far more able to deal with the situation as a man in his thirties than a boy who is 11. The most important aspect of the scenario for me, was the way the teacher reflected on his actions, to look for a better outcome, and also wanted to build a better relationship with the child.

When I visited the school a week later the teacher informed me he had spoken to the boy at the start of the next lesson. He said, it only took a couple of minutes as the other children were lining up outside his class after break. He called the student in and explained that he wasn't in any trouble (as he could see the anxiety on the boy's face after their altercation the previous day), he just wanted to go through what had happened the previous day. The teacher started by asking, what had he, as a teacher, done to deserve the names he was called? (Asked in an enquiring non-threatening and calm way.) The boy said he hadn't done anything to deserve it, he just wanted to shut him up as he was being annoying. The teacher then said that he recognised that he himself had been annoyed as well, so they could both learn from the situation as it would be better if they didn't get annoyed with each other in the future. He also mentioned to the boy about his maturity and ability and wanted to make sure he did the best for him, and finished the discussion with, 'So, let's try to be a bit better with each other – agreed?' They agreed, and the lovely thing was the teacher said to me, 'It only took a couple of minutes to sort it out and it worked!' The nice final point was, later in the day, without any prompting, the boy had written a letter to apologise.

These are the signs of a very good teacher, and well worth copying. Not only did he recognise when he had not been at his best, but he was brave enough to admit this to a student as well.

De-escalation and diversion

Being in control of yourself at all times will mean you will be able to look at alternatives to the situations you find yourself in. For example, the use of jokes (as long as they are funny and avoid any sarcasm) when a harsh comment is made. The tone you use will always be important and the total avoidance of any sarcasm is crucial. You are aiming to engage in a conversation and move towards a good solution to any situation. Be relaxed and de-escalate the situation, making comments such as, 'Wow that sounded harsh, what shall we do about this situation?', using a caring enquiring tone. You will recognise what works as you improve using different alternatives. Roll with the comments; if they want to wrestle, then turn it into a dance.

One technique I always teach teachers is what is known as the 'fish and chip shop solution'. I have written about it in the past but is always worth repeating.

When you have to speak with a child or student outside of the classroom, you have to recognise you have caused the situation to escalate in the mind of the one asked to come with you. In doing so they are now using more of their emotional part of their limbic system: fight, flight, flock or freeze. None of these approaches allow them to think about the situation in hand or to consider alternative approaches and courses of actions when returning to the class. So, you need to move their brain, to stop them being emotional and responding accordingly and to use more of their hippocampus, remembering good things and returning to being calm. You can do so by asking them when they get outside, after thanking them for coming with you, 'Do you know of a good fish and chip shop around here?' Immediately, not only by your quizzical tone, but also by the nature of the question, it requires them to think differently about the new situation they find themselves in. If you then quickly follow it up with, 'I usually turn left at the gate and I haven't found one yet, which one do you use and do you like fish and chips?' The quick fire questions on this topic causes them to have to think of a fish and chip shop, food, which way do they go home, along with a variety of other thoughts that are popping into their heads, which have nothing to do with the incident in the room or the situation they expected to find themselves in once they have come outside. Once they have answered one or two questions relating to the fish and chip shop, or other spurious questions, you can ask them, in the same inquisitive tone, 'What was going on in there?' You will then get a far more thoughtful answer and on a lot of occasions you will get an apology as they start to explain. At this point, bear in mind it will have something to do with the 3Ms, so check things are ok with them as well as what's going on in their lives, do they understand the work and is there anything you can do to help, and also do they understand why they are doing it? Some of their answers may need you to have a longer chat with them at a more appropriate time, or even involve others, but at least you have helped them handle a situation which was getting out of their control.

It is far easier and more beneficial to engage with someone when you have created a calm, non-threatening atmosphere which these questions aim to do. Also, once you have dealt with the situation, you must then organise their re-entry to the classroom. Ask them who will want to talk to them when they get back in, to see what has been said? Then ask them, what they are going to do when they do speak to that person, so as not to make them get into trouble? Then ask them is there anything you can do to help in the situation, or will they manage to keep things under control? They invariably say they will manage, at which point you have a chance to thank them for the chat and to say how impressed you are with their attitude.

This technique of deflecting their thoughts by asking random questions is of course a great way to take their minds off the current situation. This can also be used when you notice someone is becoming too distracted, by asking them to do a simple job for you or asking them about something fairly random first and then re-directing them back to the task in hand. Dealing with situations head on by tackling what you are witnessing or hearing without first appreciating what emotional state the person is in who you are addressing will maintain the person in the emotional state. You are always seeking to use a far more constructive part of their brain so they can regain control and manage themselves better.

For one or two students whom you know struggle with being within a classroom and could perhaps benefit with a little work, I have seen the technique of taking some books or delivering a message to a colleague work very effectively. For some, if the books are heavy, they act as a hug to the senses as they hold them tight and this also adds to the calming effect of a walk.

Behaviour is a living out of the situation in front of you at any one moment and knowing this can help you be in charge of the environment and what they are a part of, then their behaviour is for them to manage and control.

The younger the person the easier deflection works; the older they become then conversation and engagement works better. But the one thing that works best of all is when you remain calm and have built a good relationship with them in the first place.

Chapter 9

Strategies for miscellaneous school activities

The experiences that you will encounter during your teaching career will be many and varied. The academic progress of those in the classroom is just one part of the role you have signed up for. You are also going to be involved in the emotional and social development of young people, trying to meet the expectations of parents and fellow colleagues as well as being involved in a range of challenges and opportunities. The more that you become involved in the life of the school the more your skills will also develop in the classroom as they will involve responsibility, communication, various aspects of leadership and management as well as working with other staff members.

Some of these responsibilities might involve you having to overcome your own fears, such as speaking to a large group of adults or taking responsibility for students outside of the school. Here are a few thoughts to bear in mind as you take on three of the main opportunities that come your way.

Delivering talks/training to staff members

Before the talk

Your preparation is going to be key to the success of the delivery.

Before you embark on any talk you must have a thorough knowledge about the subject to be discussed. This should include background knowledge, why it is important and relevant for the people that you are speaking to, as well as offering practical advice about how they can implement the things you are talking about. In short: *make it relevant.*

When delivering a talk, you are not only imparting information, but you are also aiming to engage the audience so as to keep their attention and the best way to do this is to provide them with opportunities to contribute as soon as you can. Within the first few slides if using a power point presentation ask them for their opinion or experience regarding the topic you are discussing. *Make it engaging.*

Be aware of your body language as well as the tone of your voice. Part of the presentation is in actual fact, you. The more you appear confident, smiling and making eye contact the more the audience will relax. Your words need to be heard by everyone so project your voice to the person on the back row. If possible, move up and down the stage so that you are causing the audience to pay attention to you. Hand movements should be kept within the middle box of your torso and used to emphasis points. Open hand gestures are always relaxing, non-threatening and help emphasis your confidence to the audience. *At all times inspire confidence.*

Handling your nerves can be difficult and there are some common issues that tend to creep in when people are nervous – these are often used to try to build a sympathetic link with the audience. It never works! So please don't say things like:

> *I am nervous.*
> *This is the first time I have done anything like this.*
> *I hope the IT works.*

If things do go wrong with the IT (which is inevitable, they will do at some point!), accept that things have gone wrong and either fix the problem or ask someone to come and sort it. The technicians should be approached and at least be on hand as you start. Test the presentation before you start but always be ready for the unexpected so if it arrives be confident that you know the subject and control your body language. Your calm approach will overcompensate for any mishaps. The more you practice, the easier it will be on the day. If you can prepare your words in your head like an actor prepares for a play, then so much the better. Accept you might have sleepless nights before and that you may feel sick before the event. Nerves play their part in making sure you do it right. You will get better the more you do. Also, the skills you need for the stage are the same as within the classroom, so get used to watching yourself and your mannerisms in the classroom and hone your skills there ready for when you have a different audience. If people ask you how you feel about giving the talk one useful tip is to exchange the word 'nervous' for 'excited', so you say, 'I am excited about giving the talk'. This will make a surprising difference to how you feel. *Manage your nerves.*

Organising trips

The chance to become involved in trips should be looked upon as a wonderful opportunity to get to know the children or students better. Once they are free from the usual confines of school, they tend to act in a more relaxed way and reveal more of their character and personality. It is also a good opportunity to speak with them about their lives, likes, dislikes, family and future in a casual manner without the time constraints that school imposes. There will be the necessary educational aspect that needs to be fulfilled but along with that there is a greater opportunity for you to impact upon their social and emotional development. So how do you make sure that the time is well spent in these areas so that you will see the benefit of it when you return to the classroom?

Maximising the opportunities

Autonomy

The schools I have worked with invariably tell the children and students before the trip the expected behaviour that they all must adhere to. If the trip involves an overnight stay then these instructions will also include how they should look after their rooms, what time the lights should go out, and that they should show general respect for the premises they are visiting. All the points are valid and important and will help with the smooth running of the trip. To help make this become a learning experience I advise that you allow the students and children to draw up the list of what they think they all should do. Spend time with them discussing all the above areas and see who comes up with what, then explore their ideas and the reasoning behind their ideas. It is a great group work activity.

I have always found that when you involve them they are far more strict than adults ever would be to start with, but over the time of the discussion they recognise their behaviour is their responsibility and the smooth running of the whole trip happens when they all take responsibility for their own actions and support one another.

You can also ask them what role adults should have in making sure things work well, or when the agreed rules don't work. Once they have reached Year 3 they like to have more responsibility and autonomy for themselves as they learn social responsibility, so looking for times for this to happen is important. We learn from our mistakes and this includes social ones as well so be aware that whilst on the trip some will have opportunities to learn and reassess what they have done and look for ways to make it better next time. Control should be as much as possible given to them and whilst under your watchful eye you can see how well they cope. Giving out too many rules and guidelines before the event takes away the learning opportunities presented by the trip.

Transference

The academic side of the trip is always quite rightly emphasised and the learning always transferred back into the classroom, but also watch for any social and emotional skills that a young person demonstrates, including encouragement, support, kindness, initiative and inquisitiveness, and help them recognise how they could use those skills back in the classroom as well. Help them see how they can use the skills not only to help themselves but also their friends.

As they show you their personality, look for the positive aspects of it that please you and that you know will be a part of making them into a nice adult, then praise and comment about it to them. Help them see that you notice them as a person and are pleased for what they are becoming. You will see the impact this will have on them as not only are you helping them know themselves better but you are also helping them widen the areas they can impact, by being a nice person.

Providing feedback – coaching others

Lesson observations and providing feedback will over time become part of the norm, especially as you progress within your teaching career. This is often a source of discord and frustration with many teachers as they often dislike the process which is in fact meant to help improve their skills.

The first point to remember is:

Think about your own experiences and how feedback or coaching made you feel. What was the most positive aspect of it and what had the most impact? Try to unpick what was the reason it helped you and weave that approach into the way you coach others. Copy only the good points!

The second point to remember is:

All teachers that I speak to evaluate their own lessons in one form or another and the excellent ones evaluate themselves through constantly monitoring an almost inexhaustible list such as: the pace of the lesson, the time on the clock, the individual and whole classroom engagement, the learning, the class environment, the pupil premium student as well as the gifted and talented student, the SEND student, the understanding of the topic, the teaching assistant, the temperature, themselves, the follow up .... Can you see that the list goes on and on and this list grows with experience and confidence over time?

Your approach therefore is your chance to examine and look for ways for the person to improve their own critical view of themselves, to improve on the list of questions that they use, and to find ways that they can explore possibilities to improve their own teaching after doing so. Check to see what they already reflect upon and ask them what areas they would wish to improve on. You will no doubt have the answers and have seen lots of ways to help. It would seem strange if you don't, yet remember they will be served better if they are allowed to discover their own weaknesses through exploring questions and reflecting and then start to explore possible ways they could overcome them. Giving answers just gives answers; asking questions and exploring ideas develops learning.

When a person is struggling then the evaluations and reflection tend to have got stuck at a certain point. The level of stress within the teacher at this point prevents them looking at the whole, as they narrow their focus on the thing causing the stress without recognising that this one thing may in fact have an impact upon lots of other things. Stress narrows creativity and possibilities within us so our role in helping people should start with helping them relax and look at the possibilities and achievements. I recently spoke to one teacher who was struggling with a group of 14-year-olds within the class who were constantly off task and disruptive and only ever did a small piece of work. I highlighted that in fact they had already done well as this was one class where they stayed for the whole time, so the teacher was already more successful here than other classes when the students didn't even turn up! Also, the students had been engaged even if it was in a small way and had listened to instructions even if they only then did a small piece of work. The hard work had been done in that the relationship had already started to form; the next task was to help them stay more focused. We then looked at what the teacher already knew about the students and I also asked who were the ones staying on task and what was the teacher doing for them? The session revolved around me asking him to explore the whole class and look at the whole lesson. As the saying goes, 'How do you eat an elephant? One bite at a time.' I encouraged the teacher to see what small steps they could perhaps do. What is it they want to achieve and how much have the students been involved in talking about what it is he is wanting to do for them that makes the lesson meaningful? Solving problems sometimes takes time and patience.

The third point to remember is:

Problems come with being alive. I often say if you are alive you have a problem or an issue that needs addressing; the two go hand in hand. But it's not the problems that define us, it's how we tackle them that shows our character and worth and when coaching and mentoring others this should always be the starting point from the premise that the problems and issues are the learning blocks to improvement and the harder they are the more we are going to learn.

You may well have the answers and the solutions and viewpoints on the situation, and these may all be valid and could possibly solve the situation, yet as a coach or when providing feedback to someone you are going to be serving them well if you help them develop questions and explore solutions for themselves. Steer them and guide them to areas they may not have thought about and when they have arrived encourage them to explore options with this new outlook.

To build up this skill first with yourself, get used to asking questions of yourself and reflecting on what you have done each day. Check your motives, your input, your drive, your aim and the result of your effort and see if it fits in with your own philosophy on life and the personal vision you have. Model yourself on who you want to be. Become your best coach and mentor but also your own best friend as you understand your own limitations and weaknesses. Be honest and encourage others to do the same as you mentor and coach them. It helps that we know ourselves well, which brings us to the next chapter.

Chapter 10

Strategies for school policies and procedures, induction and new students' arrivals

School policies and procedures

It is important to integrate yourselves into the workings of the school in which you work as soon as possible and your first few days are key in familiarising yourself to the way the school works and its ethos. No doubt one of the reasons you have chosen to work there in the first place is because of the people you have already met as well as the location and catchment of the children you are seeking to teach. I am always pleasantly surprised about the many reasons teachers have for why they work at a particular school. One of the main ones often given to me is that they love the type of children they will be working with. Without doubt this is an encouraging attitude as the commitment needed to work with some children and students to help them achieve all they can will often involve a lot of emotional input, as well as all the skills and techniques you can provide to teach the subject. It will be very important that your time there is meaningful for you. On top of that there is the model and manageable parts of the school which will help enable you to fulfil what is meaningful and this will be the many school policies and procedures in place so the school can function.

The policies will cover a number of different areas, including statutory regulations and guidelines, health and safety, school improvement, special educational needs, community, curriculum and early years. As you can appreciate the list is extensive! These policies are in place so that you will have a set of established expectations for specific behaviour during the normal daily life of the school, so as to make the school a safe and effective place to learn and help with the interaction between the school, the pupils, the parents as well as the community. They are also there to address the practical implications of how to work towards the whole school vision, and to ensure that the day-to-day actions based on the decisions made are in line with the vision. I hope you appreciate the importance of getting to know the policies that have an immediate effect upon how you are going to achieve your aim of being effective within the school. No doubt the school will inform you about the typical daily expectations of your role and the parts you will need to know immediately. Some policies are also going to have more relevance to you, such as the school's safeguarding policy, which will help you to know and understand your role to enable the children and students to stay safe. You will also be introduced to the safeguarding team, photos of whom are often displayed around the school so everyone knows who has the specific responsibility for this area.

On top of the many policies you will hear about you will also be introduced to the many procedures the school has for you to follow. The difference quite simply is the policies are non-negotiable, change very rarely, have widespread implications and very broadly explain the what and the why. The procedures, however, tend to have a more narrow focus, are subject to change and continued improvement and cover more of the how, who, when, and provide you with a far more detailed descriptions of activities.

Behaviour policy and procedure

One of the first questions a lot of teachers have is about the behaviour policy and procedure. What happens when a child does something not considered the school or classroom norm? What steps should you take when things do happen? I am always struck by the two differing approaches to this. There are those who always want to follow the behaviour procedure when things don't go right and those who never seem to ever refer to it. You will have to make up your own mind about what to do in the best interest of the child, the students, the school and yourself. They are there as a guide and assistance should you need to use them. The ultimate aim is for you as a teacher is to have the children and students following the school norm and rules. This book is aiming to equip you to look beyond the actions you witness to find the reason as to why the actions occurred and then help correct the behaviour accordingly with this new understanding so all can move on and learn, doing their best to maintain a positive relationship whilst doing so.

Often, rigid adherence to policy and procedure associated with behaviour can have a negative effect not only upon the person on the receiving end of it but also on the one implementing it. Consequences of actions should be used, as this helps children and students to understand their social responsibility. You will also discover when discretion is also the better policy to adopt. When you take this option with a child or student, let them know that you are using your discretion and it is for once only for the purpose of them learning from the experience. I would always advocate keeping those around you aware of what you are doing and seeking their advice and guidance so as to stay on track with the school ethos and vision. You are part of a wider team and this is always to be borne in mind as you work within the parameters of your chosen school. Build up your own set of skills for maintaining the correct behaviour within your area of influence. Remember the most powerful message you can give to someone who you have a good relationship with when they have done something wrong is to say to them, 'I am disappointed in you.' The starting point is of course to build those good relationships.

So the policies and procedures are there to help you and, as such, some of the issues that I see within classrooms, regarding mobile phones, uniform or make up, can be resolved by consistently adhering to the school's policy and procedures. When these are not consistently adhered to then children have a wonderful ability to notice and take advantage of those who are inconsistent. I would advocate from day one giving constant remainders and reinforcing those key policies that are aimed at bringing order and a recognised model into the lives of the children and students. It is understandable that at various times they will want to buck against the basic rules which they see as imposed upon them by adults. Yet your role is to stick to the rules, to help the students recognise their social responsibility and also to help them to be a part of the school to enable them to find a sense of belonging. The way you do so is to speak in a calm and casual manner, being persistent and consistent, following up on any discrepancy. This will pay dividends in the long run and will also, if used properly, provide you with opportunities to talk with and enquire as to the reason why they keep on wishing not to follow the school's guidelines. Some of the reasons you can explore within this book; others you will add yourself, because of the answers you will receive. Remember at all times that relationships are key.

Mobile phone policy and procedure

The issue of the use of mobile phones within schools is one area in which schools have different policies and procedures. The important thing is for you to follow what you have been told. Because phones have cameras as well as recording devices, there are a number of safeguarding aspects that have to be considered, along with the usual issues relating to the fact that phones are in effect mobile computers accessing the internet.

For some schools, confiscating a mobile phone if it is seen by a teacher in a class has become the norm. This has led unfortunately to a number of escalating incidents, especially as Generation Z have grown up with their mobile devices, and the habit of constantly checking and using the phone is far more ingrained than in previous generations. For a student to hand over their phone to someone else causes high levels of anxiety, far higher than in previous generations. Be aware of this should you have to do any confiscating.

If your school has a strict phones policy, here is a way to help you avoid it escalating out of control.

Those you are responsible for within your class need to know what you are expecting and what you are going to do about it if the school's directive is not followed by any student. Highlight your desire to avoid this happening and that you really want them to keep their phones as you know how important phones are to them. They need to work with you as both you and they have a responsibility to fit in with how the school wishes to operate. Ask them what happens if they go to the cinema? They should be able to explain to you the reminder to turn the phone off, as well as the fact that it is illegal to record any part of the film. If you are able to have the same ring tone that is used at the start of each lesson as a reminder this would work well.

If you can, introduce a shoe box for storing mobile phones for the duration of the lesson should anyone feel they might forget and be tempted to go to their phone. You can have it decorated very simply with pictures of phones of all makes. If no one wants to use the box, then it will be used if anyone accidently goes to their phone. Let them know this is your way of working with them so phones don't become an issue.

If it unfortunately does go wrong, just go over what you have already said and highlight the fact that the next time it happens you will have no alternative but to use the sanctions imposed by the school. When dealing with persistent young offenders I let them know they had no second chances – we'd already had a discussion highlighting the amount of second and third chances they had been given in the past that didn't seem to have worked, so with me it was one strike and you are out. For a new group I am usually more lenient but just as aware that I could be helping them form the habit of only learning a lesson after they have used up their chances, and I would prefer that they learnt from the discussion. Learn from you own experience. It's their responsibility if they keep or don't keep their phones as you have made them fully aware of the consequences. Having it as part of the lesson starting procedure helps also to build up a model of expectations within your class.

Tell them to put their phones away in a bag so they won't be distracted by them should they start going off in their pocket. If after all these warnings they still get their phone out then I would approach them with the shoe box and expect them to put the phone in it for the duration of the rest of the lesson. Place the box in front of them in a casual manner for them to put their phone inside. Keep the box in full view at the front of the class so they know where it is at all times.

Most of the rules that you know may cause areas of conflict can be dealt with in a similar fashion, by highlighting what you are going to do to help them get it right and then they have a responsibility to work with you as well so they don't have to face any consequences should they forget or get it wrong. The more information as to your expectations the better. Asking them for advice regarding any issue that they get into trouble with and how you can help them is also a good way to introduce some form of autonomy into their lives.

Induction

On top of the policies and procedures within school you will have to familiarise yourself with, you will also receive an induction pack or have a designated person who will help you settle into the school. All schools are busy places and the day-to-day issues that need immediate attention are many and varied. Be prepared for your best laid plans to be changed at the last minute because of some emergency or other, staff absence, information that needs your attention, conversations that change the course of your thoughts and plans. The picture I am painting is that schools are very fluid places. There will be a set timetable with set duties and set times for reports and marking and meetings and planning and the list goes on. There is always the unexpected, so expect it always!

The point I am making is they may have set you a person who is meant to look after you and make sure your induction is informative and beneficial. Yet I have known those plans go awry in the first few days because of some other issue that takes precedence. Therefore, have in mind what you want to know and use your initiative if needed to go and find the information yourself. Be proactive in learning and finding out. Make a list of anything new you wish to know at the end of the day and see how quickly you can find out about it either from the person helping you or from some other quarter. Students and children are a great source of information and insight and you asking them questions will help build up their own self esteem as well as help with your relationships. Getting to know all the acronyms within the teaching profession will take time, and there are a number of websites explaining most of the popular ones. There are hundreds! One of the first things you will have to find out about are the staff names, as most schools just use initials which can be tricky when you first start. If the school is able to supply you with photographs of the staff it will help in putting faces to names when you are in the staff room. All these things will help prepare you mentally for what is going to be an amazingly busy introduction into the working life of schools. Plan what you can that will make your life easy and prepare as much as possible. Set a mission to learn about specific areas of interest to you and seek help as much as you can. I always encourage any new starter to a school to make a list of what was helpful in the induction and what was missed out. Pass this completed list on to whoever is responsible for preparing the induction if they are interested, as you might have experienced or needed to know about something they might have overlooked or taken for granted. You can also refer to this list come the time that you yourself might be required to assist a new arrival.

Arrival of new students

Students arriving constantly will also be an issue you will have to contend with and here are a few things to consider.

New students have all the same feelings of nerves, trepidation and uncertainty as you had when you first arrived at school. They also have the added disadvantage of not only being less mature and less able to access the higher functioning part of their brain which will helps them manage their emotions, but they also may have other emotional hurdles to overcome – such as language barriers, new friends, new culture, new social area, having to manage the travelling into school, learning where everything is, rules, expectations, levels of learning, different food, temperature. It is also important to remember they may not have had a choice in the move. It may have come about for a number of reasons and not all of them positive. Some schools who are used to the fluidity of numbers and unexpected new arrivals have a programme to help assess the students' ability and access to learning before they are integrated into everyday school life. Others may not have the ability to do this and for some the transition can become very rapid. Whatever the method your school has in place it will be as well for you to be prepared for this to happen, and that the arrival of new students will change the dynamics within your often, settled class. The sense of belonging is key for any person to access the full ability of their IQ, so the speed in which you can build a relationship with any new students is going to be key, and the more this is done around school the better.

When a new student arrives in your class it is really helpful if, during the first few moments of the lesson when they arrive, you can make some introductions. When meeting your class at the door you can speak to the new person and have a quick word about your intention to introduce them to the class, and vice versa. Then everyone can say a quick name check and say hello. This could be done over registration. Each student could then add where they live as they say their name, or if they walk to school, come on the bus or are driven in. See if the new person is happy to say something as well, or if not, you can do the introductions for them. Have them sitting with you first to check their level of understanding and education to date – this will give you some idea as to the best place to sit them within the rest of the class. Check the arrangements at home before setting any homework. Think about how it takes time to settle into a new home and provide a few days' grace if possible, then make arrangements for them to catch up within school with you if at all possible. It might require you to do more work to start with but this will be repaid in the long run.

If the person has moved school because of behavioural reasons be aware that for the first few days, or even a week, the person tends to manage well as the new surroundings are enough for them to contend with and the poor behaviour diminishes. Unfortunately, students tend to revert to type once the normal expectations of school life resume and perhaps the deficiencies in their education are once again highlighted and they resort to their poor behaviour as a cover. So, you have a few days to speak with and impress on them your ability to help them with the things they struggle with, but it will require them deciding to work with you. Seek their agreement and also ask them straight, do they wish you to help and work with them. You need verbal commitment from them as soon as possible and this requires them to explain to you in the best words they can the reason they want to get it right. A simple yes is not good enough, you want to know the reason as to why they say yes. The reason they give you will be used as the point of reference for making them try – in effect it becomes the meaningful part in their life to do the hard work necessary. We often assume people want to get it right, and this may be true. It is just the struggle and inability in their own self that prevents this from becoming a reality. Therefore, your assistance could be the key to unlock spiralling poor behaviour and negative consequences. The talks you have should be relayed back to the pastoral support team and any mentor who has been assigned to the student. The more people working with them the better. These talks only need to take one or two minutes. The student will be able to understand your intention and care, and this alone for some will help. You also need to be aware that some students want to continue in their poor behaviour as they have an alternative end in sight. One student told me they wanted to get excluded as they had their eye on another school where they had their friends. The other school was a pupil referral unit, and the student thought the best way to get there was to get thrown out of the one they had been moved to. Such a short-sighted negative attitude is often understandable when you listen to the experiences they have had in the past, and for some this is their way of feeling they are in charge of their lives. Your talks will have an impact still, and will let them know you are there for them, to help them should they wish to seek an alternative more beneficial way forward for their long-term life.

Whatever the reason they are with you, remember also to make sure they know where they are going to be going after your lesson. The anxiety of them finding the next lesson will start about twenty minutes before the end of the one they are in so the earlier you can deal with this issue the better.

These are a few points to bear in mind for yourself and others. Let your anxiety be a trigger for how others are feeling as well. Be sensitive, caring and thoughtful as well as being prepared as much as possible. You will undoubtedly find things that are wrong – if you don't, please let me know as I haven't met the perfect school and would like to visit!

Chapter 11

Strategies for leadership
of other adults

At some point within your teaching career, if you are looking for promotion or overseeing your classroom with the support of a teaching assistant, you will arrive at the situation where you will be responsible for the leadership and management of other adults. With this in mind there are a few points I would like you to consider. These are in no way exhaustive but, as in the other chapters, it might help to lay down a few principles that will enable you to start on the right track.

Leadership as well as teaching are intrinsically an emotional experience and the skills you will learn within the classroom can and should be transferred into your leadership and oversight of adults. The same expectations should be also employed: high expectations; commitment and resilience to getting the task done; support and empathy for others; as well as an honest approach to the amount of time and effort that has been employed to do the task.

A good rule of thumb is to check that you use the same words when outlining your expectations both for the adults as well as the children and students that you teach.

The same should be said regarding how you deal with situations when things go well as well as when they don't. It will seem strange at first when having to highlight to an adult that they have fallen below your standards but please be assured this is the role you have taken on and those who know they have not met your expectations will recognise your authority to point out to them your disappointment. Your opening statement to check their understanding of the situations could be. 'Why do you think I wanted to have a chat with you?' This also could be used in your classroom as well as your office. Hopefully, to avoid such situations, here are a few steps for you to use as a foundation on which to build.

Step one: Creating a vision

Leadership involves you creating a vision around the work you are seeking to do and then getting the people to work with you to achieve the vision. Management is making sure that the day-to-day operation is in line with the vision. People need to know specifically the role you have set them as well as the way you wish to work to accomplish that goal. I spoke with a primary school teacher yesterday who asked what she should do with a teaching assistant who wasn't doing the things she expected her to do. She was told the TA was very experienced and had worked within the school for years and she assumed she would automatically do the things she expected.

Starting as you want to go on is key, but if, as on this occasion, setting a vision and expectations hasn't been done, then arrange a chat with the person you are working with, review how effective the time together has been and then propose a fresh approach, but this time outline it around the vision you have now created. Highlight how things should work in the future and what you, as well as the team or individual, will need to do differently in order to accomplish the vision. Keep repeating the aims and vision so that they become part of the everyday thinking of everybody. If your aim is to raise standards for all, then keep highlighting every small step that works towards this from what has taken place within the day.

Step two: Personal values

Your personal values and principles should be understood and adhered to at all times and woven into the environment and work ethic you aim to lead.

Why should anyone be led or taught by you? What makes you worth listening to and learning from? What are your personal strengths and the best thing about you as a person? In the section on understanding self we examine this in more detail. This is an item often overlooked within the business of life but is an important aspect not only in the way you can inspire others but also in helping to create a work environment that people can feel safe in and belong to. It also brings a touch of personality to the workforce, so they get to know you better.

Think about how you like your classroom environment. How do you like them to work, talk to each other, engage in learning? What are the aspects of it that you enjoy? Try to weave these into how you lead adults as well. If your aim is to enable those in the classroom to enjoy learning and discovery, encourage your staff to also seek for ways they can learn and discover things about their work or role that will improve how you want things to develop.

Step three: Communication

When communicating with others, always include praise and personal recognition. People are more than the consequences of their actions. People like to be recognised and appreciated for who they are and what they personally bring to the workplace and the school. Most people that are employed within the educational system work there because they care for the children and the students contained within it and are concerned about doing a good job for them. With this in mind, look for things that the staff do which make the children and students' lives better on the emotional and social side as well as the academic, and communicate your thanks and recognition for what they are doing.

Communication is better face to face as so many more messages are conveyed through tone, body language, facial expressions than can ever be communicated through an email no matter how many emojis you put in them. Always ask yourself. Can I go and find them to say this rather than sending them an email? Make face to face your primary form of communication every time you can, with email being your second choice. I have stood in the corridor at a school when two people were on the phone to each other but no more than twenty feet apart! I could hear both sides of the conversation regarding which week are we on when we come back after half term. Walking is good, smiling is good, communication face to face is good. Use those good times when you can.

Your communication should also be an opportunity for you to pass on your thanks for what they do, who they are and what they bring to the classroom and the team. 'Thanks for all you do. I am glad you work with me. It's a pleasure working with you. Thanks for what you bring to the team.' These comments should be heartfelt and genuine. They are also the glue that will keep the team together through the difficult times.

Step four: Inspire confidence

As a leader you will be on show to those you seek to lead; they will be watching your reaction to events and situations that you have to face. Working within schools you can guarantee that each day will provide you with new challenges and different situations that will need to be addressed and overcome: budgets, parents, governors, children, fellow staff members, new initiatives and constant scrutiny.

You will also be expected to focus sometimes on things that perhaps are not the top priority for both you and your team. You will be the one who will create how all these situations should be approached and dealt with. Never compromise on your values regardless of how you may feel or view what you are being asked to do. If you have highlighted how you want people to work, then you need to exemplify that approach every day and in every situation. Above everything, learn to inspire confidence and calm professionalism in all you do. In doing so you help others work to their best and become the role model that encourages others to follow you.

Step five: Dealing with poor performance

One of the topics I continually get asked to cover with leaders in schools is how to have the difficult conversation. It may be for a variety of reasons, ranging from poor performance, negative attitude towards others and the school, absenteeism, lack of commitment to the culture and life of the school, or rude and sarcastic comments towards others. These are issues you can expect to have to deal with if you have taken on the role of leadership. Read the list again and see if I am talking about students, children or adults? I hope you will notice that all of these issues can be attributed towards all of these groups. Which brings me back to the point that you will be learning how to have difficult conversations with adults because you should be having them on a regular basis with students and children within your classroom or in your daily work around school.

The comment I often receive is that it is different with adults. I appreciate that the adults may have a more practised and belligerent attitude than some of the children and it's impossible to call their parents to have a word with them. But it is still the case that they have fallen below the expected standards.

You should tackle conversations with adults with the same amount of commitment, care and understanding to seek why the problem is occurring and what you as a leader can do to help overcome the situation so that things can move forward in a more positive manner.

Your relationship with them in all situations is key.

Help them see any inconsistencies and remind them of what they have shared with you in the past and how they can use those values and purpose to overcome the issue you are needing to address now.

The other point to remember is when you first meet them and have highlighted your vision you should include the way you would like the team to work. Once you have done this ask them if they all agree. My philosophy is 'Excellence and Fun'. Those are the two things I look for within work, teams and with every interaction with those I come into contact with. I spend time explaining how those two things should be experienced and embedded as we seek to work together towards the vision I emphasise. I then ask for their commitment towards this, knowing that those words will be the words I challenge myself by in my daily work but also theirs as they are now a vital part of my team.

You should also be able to say what it is you expect and establish buy-in to this from everyone. This then provides you with the base line for challenging, rewarding and encouraging those you seek to lead to live by.

They should know what you expect, and they should also know when they have delivered as well as when they have not, and your comments should always be challenging and encouraging at all times when you meet them. With this approach the difficult conversation does not stand alone, isolated from the norm, becoming something which has to be tackled – it is just another conversation that is taking place as you all work to deliver the vision agreed upon. For adults, just as in the classroom, seek first and foremost before any situation arises to build a strong relationship based upon mutual understanding and respect. I mentioned at the start of this section one conversation starter, another approach is to ask the person 'How do you think you come across to others? What impression are you seeking to give to the students and the rest of the team?' Be inquisitive as this is often a question that folks haven't given a lot of thought to. As a leader seek to learn more about those you are leading. Asking them questions about themselves and the reasons as to why they do things or don't do things is often a great starting point to finding alternative strategies to arrive at a better outcome. Which brings us onto the next point.

Step six: Knowing your staff

In light of what has been said, people who fall below the expected standards usually have a reason for the dip. This may be personal or work related and it's important to know what extenuating circumstances they may be facing that could be affecting their overall effectiveness. This means knowing your staff as best you can. Praise and acknowledgment mean different things to different people. Some like personal recognition others just want to be appreciated for what they do. Others like to share personal items to build a bond whilst others only share things related to work and keep their private life private. Some like to talk and explore ideas; others like to be told what to do and are not interested in exploring ideas. Some will always give their opinion and others will need to be asked. The way you like to be led, spoken to and encouraged may be the same for others but often not all. The more you appreciate the differences the better it will be to connect with them and the more they will like to have you as their leader. Your classroom will be made up of individuals with all their different experience and expectations and you know you have to differentiate, provide scaffolded learning at times and adapt your resources to the needs of the individual. In doing so you are able to get the best out of all of them. Likewise, with the adults, find out how they like to be led, encouraged and dealt with and do your best to work with them.

As you will have more time to talk with the staff you will lead, find out what it is that they value about their work, themselves as a person and why they are doing the job in the first place. Look for the motivating factor within their lives that makes coming to school worthwhile. The more you know about them the easier it will be for you to challenge them in light of their values and the way they do their work should a problem arise, as well as making working for you meaningful by linking it to their personal aims and ambition.

Step seven: Admit your mistakes

Leading as well as everything else you will do within school will get better through experience. Yet we know that we learn through our mistakes just as much as through our success so the chances are you will make mistakes in both your method of teaching and managing and leading students just as you will with adults. It will be wise to admit when you recognise those mistakes and seek to show how you are going to alter your approach and learn from them. It is also a good idea to make sure that you keep communication open well enough so that the people you lead have the opportunity to let you know if they think you are doing things wrong. Humility along with integrity are two very necessary elements that you should seek to preserve during your time as a leader. Check on how you are doing. This is always a good question to ask of those you lead, in the classroom as a teacher, as a co-worker with a TA, or as a leader of a team. You need to know how good you are and aim to improve, just as you ask of those around you.

I asked folks on my Facebook page what aspects of leadership they think are most important and the responses I had from people included: humility, respect given and earned, enthusiasm, integrity, sense of humour, listening, vision, clarity, service, trust, belief, empathy, honesty, fairness.

It's a wonderful list, and as you can see it involves a good deal of emotional attachment. This comes first before any outstanding work can be done. Enjoy the role and treat all those under your care with all of the above.

PART 3

Specific strategies for everyday use

Chapter 12

Strategies on specific issues for everyday classroom use

Introduction

Relationships are key for you to be able to teach effectively and the strategies throughout this book will highlight some of the many issues that children and young people are facing daily within their lives. How you help them whilst they are in your lesson, as well as how you coach and mentor them on their behaviour, wll help cement good positive relationships. The students and children may exhibit more stress within your lesson simply because you are asking them to deal with learning new things, and this could be the catalyst for them to react. Having them taken out of the lessons is one way to help reduce stress, yet they need to be in your lesson in order to learn. So, you need to play your part in reducing the stress levels by getting to know and understand them. Finding effective strategies to help them to cope with life is going to be key in you becoming a successful teacher. Your aim is not to manage their behaviour but to help them find solutions, so they have the skills to manage their own behaviour.

The behaviour you see before you is often the best coping mechanism they have for a situation they don't think they can handle, or it may be a way of trying to make their own life and situation easier. It can often be the case that a reasonable request from you may well be the straw that breaks the camel's back, resulting in you being on the receiving end of the full response built up from many hours or days of pent up frustration. You are constantly going to have to examine your approach and response to these situations, and it is often not as clear as you like to think. All behaviour will have consequences, and this is often part of the lesson the young person or student needs to learn to help establish a better approach. The use of punishment as a form of learning has very limited – if any – success and tends to move people away from a positive relationship. Behaviour and social etiquette are to be learned and when these are not present, they need to be taught. Just like in a lesson, if a student hasn't managed to learn what is being explained you need to try a different approach until they understand and can move on. I am yet to see maths knowledge improved by punishment or detentions. So, with social and emotional skills, well directed intervention, help, coaching and guidance tends to reap a reward and this is what I am advocating. The length of time that you spend asking questions and trying to find the root cause of the behaviour you see in front of you will never be wasted and will I believe be less time consuming than having to issue detentions and call parents to assist in behaviour management. Keep your questions short and targeted and always see yourself as someone exploring reasons and possibilities so as to get to know your students better.

The chapters before will have provided a good starting point, yet you will always have to recognise that the young people you teach come from various backgrounds with various experiences and expectations. Their upbringing and life lessons may not have equipped them for being able to cope with the next section of their education and this will cause anxiety as well as issues that have to be overcome. You can and should help them through all of this as well as helping them grasp all the aspects of the curriculum. We can all teach well behaved children. Your skill and competence will grow as you teach those who need more from you than just the subject you teach. Young people need teachers to become teachers for the whole child not just the subject.

Schools are employing more counsellors and therapists to cope with the growing demand of issues that young people face. For the more ingrained issues you come across, their help may be needed to assist with the work you have tried to do by talking with the students and aiming to keep them within the class. It will be good if your short direct intervention opens up the dialogue between you and your students, to help them learn within your classroom, but if not then the help of counsellors and therapists should be sought. All are working for the same aim to provide students and young people with a safe and caring place to grow, develop and learn.

The following strategies are based on some typical situations you may find yourself in, and I wish you well in using them to improve your understanding of the students as well as your own teaching practice. You will see that I have tried to cover the items contained within BASE and the 3Ms – these are always a good starting point for any issue you experience. Students and young people tend to have their own reasons for what they are doing – you can help unpick those reasons with short questions that help get things back on track so as to proceed with the lesson, and they can find an alternative answer to the issues and problems they have given you. I have tried to provide you with a variety of possible reasons as to why the students may be responding in a certain way. The list is not complete and should be used as a starting point, but should, I hope, always point you in a direction that is worth exploring. The strategies that you adopt will improve your skills as a teacher and the strategies that the children and students learn from your intervention, wisdom, patience and care will improve their life chances as adults.

Scenario 1: Defiance – a student refuses to follow basic instructions and is rude in their response to you

A natural reaction on being faced with someone being rude to you is to take offence. Especially when it is someone who you naturally think should be showing you respect because of your position within school, or simply because of age. This is understandable, but you must do your utmost not to be triggered as your response needs to be one of inquisitiveness and calmness. This is simply because, if your actions leading up to the event have been measured and polite, then the response is highlighting an issue that the other person has which needs addressing and it's important to ascertain what is causing such a negative response. Consequences regarding their outburst can and should be addressed later when the person will be in a position to reflect upon their actions, but first here are some possible reasons for you to explore so as to arrive at a position of support and create the environment for their improvement. I asked a group of mixed students aged 14–15, when they were out of lesson (establishing first that I was not meaning to get them into trouble but that I was just curious), 'Where are you all meant to be at the moment?' The reply from the alpha male of the group was, 'Anywhere where you're f****** not!' At which point they all walked away from me. You have to appreciate that I was a stranger to them as I was in the school on a consultancy basis and to them I probably triggered thoughts of authority due to my dress and age. From that one interaction I was able to learn, not only the possible causes of the comment but also more about the issues the school was facing regarding some of its pupils. Needless to say I didn't follow them at that point but did speak with the alpha male on a later occasion. He wasn't too hard to identify, and I had a one-to-one chat with him for five minutes to learn more about why he chose to speak to a stranger like that, particularly when he had been told that things were ok and I wasn't getting him into trouble. The comments he made towards me didn't need for me to become emotionally engaged, aggressive or confrontational as it was just a form of communication that showed his anxiety and anger. The conclusion for him was positive. After our five-minute chat he has learnt that not everyone is out to get him and that he shouldn't write everyone off before he has got to know them. I also got an apology from him, which wasn't asked for.

Possible social and emotional causes

Age

From the ages of 8 to 15, adolescence causes individuals to reflect and question who is in charge of their lives, and they may have spells of being rebellious and aggressive. If they are surrounded by friends, they may be in the position of wanting to show off at your expense. You may in fact be a safe person on whom they can practice their rudeness, and the sooner you can help them realise – by your reaction and intervention – that the approach is both unnecessary and ineffective for achieving a positive end, the better.

Strategies

If this occurs in the classroom your opening lines need to highlight that the behaviour is unacceptable, and you need to make the call whether to deal with the situation there and then or arrange to see them later. If you want to deal with them straight away, then try to move them away from any audience by saying, 'Come with me for a moment.' Do this in a calm voice and move away, highlighting that you wish them to follow you. Then ask, 'What was that about? Why did you choose to be rude to me?' in an inquisitive tone, so that it highlights you are not annoyed or triggered by the event. Then you can start to explore some of the issues mentioned below. Or if you have to see them later say, 'You and I need to talk about your response, and I will see you at …. Now I would like you to get on with the work I have set you.' Or you could repeat the instructions again that caused the issue and then walk away to return in a few minutes to check how they are doing. Give them space and don't crowd them as they will have triggered themselves and need to reflect and calm down. Having you close will keep the tension high.

When you do get a chance to talk with them then talk about their approach to things they don't like, modelling how to deal with rudeness by your calm approach. Explain that it's not unusual for young people to challenge people or situations they don't like, it's part of growing up as they learn to be independent, but how they do so is important as it shows their character. If possible, have them reflect on their own values and character: how would they like to come across as an adult? What kind of person would they like to be? Make sure you are asking in a manner that is considering their autonomy and helping them reflect, and ensure you mention good things about them along the way. Try not to ask for an apology; the aim is for them to volunteer one. Then you can commend them for turning things around.

Home/personal life

Sometimes their aggression and defiance are manifested within school as they are unable to do so at home or within their social set up. School then becomes their release valve. You might have triggered a reminder of what they don't like at home by telling them to do things they don't want to do.

Strategy

This *may* be an area that needs looking into regarding child protection issues. Subtly check to see if things are OK outside of your classroom. (This is also a good opportunity to get to know them and build a better relationship with them.) Ask if they argue at home, and whether they have found that it works. Then if not perhaps a better approach might be ....

Relationship/belonging

They could have a poor relationship with you, the class or the lesson. The way in which you are asking them to do things could be patronising, singling out, or deemed to be unfair in their eyes. Why should they follow your rules or requests if they feel they are not cared for by you or they don't feel they belong in your class?

Strategy

People are less likely to be defiant with you if you have a good relationship with them and they feel you are treating them with respect, that you value and listen to them. Check on your relationships and affirm your task of doing your very best for them. Check also how they feel within the lesson and class, that they feel a sense of belonging not only to a few but to the class as a whole.

Self-esteem

Defiance provides them with an alternative way to examine their own low self-esteem. They may also be deflecting away from the learning task because of their lack of ability. They may be anxious that if they conform, more will then be asked of them.

Strategy

Ask how they are getting on within school and other lessons. Check also about family and friends. Their answers should highlight how they view the part they play in all of these relationships. If they are older than 15, ask for their thoughts about their own future. This will give you a good indication as to how they think about themselves. Check they are comfortable about their involvement within the class, that they have a sense of belonging.

Possible challenges to sense of coherence

Model

Something in their life is not happening in an ordered and structured way as they believe it should be. This could be in school, or within their home or social life. The constant input that students receive from social media, regarding their personal lives, means that situations can arise very quickly and affect their mood.

Strategy

Ask how they are feeling, what kind of day they are having, what their weekend was like. Look for anything that may have caused anxiety relating to change outside of the situation they find themselves in. Be aware that changes in the classroom and even potential changes cause anxiety.

Manageable

For someone who is often defiant to make the change to being compliant opens up a whole new area which they may be unsure about. They may be worried about reactions and consequences from their peers by appearing to follow your instructions. This could be what is making them feel they can't manage the situation.

Strategy

Ask if they understand what the lesson is about and check their ability to cope with the learning objective. Ask them what it is that they think is unreasonable about the request you have made. Give them time to reconsider and manage the situation better. Give them autonomy for any positive choices they make. Listen to clues in their answers to see if it highlights areas relating to possible causes. Maintain your composure at all times and reiterate that your request is all part of normal school life, that you are here for them, to help them. Maintain your relationship.

Meaningful

To follow your instructions is not meaningful for them. This could be because of peer pressure, their relationship with you, the lesson content or the impact on who they are as a person and how they view themselves.

Strategy

Check that they are OK with life in general and seek to know what they find meaningful in their lives. Family, friends, themselves? To act defiantly towards you might be meaningful to them because of the reaction from their friends, or they don't like you, or the school, the class or the lesson. Find out what they *do* like and want and see how you and the lesson can work with them to help them achieve by linking it to their interests. Listen well to their answers, it will tell you a lot about them.

Scenario 2: Name calling and being rude to each other

Possible social and emotional causes

This has become an issue in many classrooms as children and students seek to find their own identity and want to highlight differences in each other. Generation Z has become far more tolerant about diversity, such as sexuality or race, yet the issues still arise for more basic items such as personal likes and dislikes or ability to do something or not. We have always known children can be cruel and it's not hard to think back to the name calling we may have witnessed or been on the receiving end of when we were younger. Being in the right crowd is very important for some, even if the right crowd is not always the best crowd for our social and emotional health. Being a swot or a nerd, or following too closely to what the school expects, can often lead to name calling and it's important that you as a teacher create a beneficial and encouraging positive environment. Name calling can also be used as a form of bullying or intimidation and if this is not dealt with early, the name calling may escalate. Here are a few reasons why, and some ideas as to what you can explore to find a solution.

Age

This issue is unfortunately not isolated to a specific age – as we know, adults still persist in name calling and being rude to others and each other. Often closely associated with their need to dominate and hurt others, this is found throughout life. Peer pressure is at its strongest at the age of 14. They may be just copying each other as a way of strengthening their bonds to each other.

Strategy

The age of the person should be taken into account when deciding how to deal with the issue. With students of secondary school age, you could, if appropriate, include a lesson on the effects of name calling on themselves and others to try to change their attitude towards name calling. Discuss the effect and why they do it and come to an agreement trying to become more thoughtful and empathetic. You could make your classroom off limits for negative statements for one another and once that has been achieved encourage them to widen the area. With students of a younger age, take a more directed approach to individuals regarding expectations and standards and explain the values and attitudes you are wanting to see in a clear manner. Highlight when people say nice things and to each other as the preferred approach.

Home/personal life

Name calling and rudeness can often have its roots in family as well as in the choice of friends that have been made as children find identity with each other through copying. Computer games and media shows often contain material that highlight people interacting with each other in a rude offensive way, and again children looking towards role models may mistake this for appropriate behaviour.

Strategy

Get to know the parents and find out as much as you can about the influences upon the students' lives so, if necessary, you can give more targeted support and also see if the parents also find the name calling behaviour a problem. Other influences from older siblings or friends can also play a part, so check to see if more appropriate links with people with a better influence could be encouraged. Set them working with people they don't know, to learn about building relationships. If you are going to be doing this, tell them why you are going to be doing so and that you will also be asking questions at the end to see what they have learnt not only about the lesson but also about each other.

Relationship/belonging

Relationships and belonging play such a key role during school life, and behaviour associated with friends can often have a more powerful impact upon behaviour than listening to or respecting authority. Therefore, name calling can become a bonding experience for those who engage in it to the detriment of others. Also, affiliation to groups outside of school may be influencing their choice of words and hurtful comments inside school.

Strategy

Check to see what relationships the person has outside of the area of contact you have with them. Help to find ways during the lessons to discover different things about each other and to be curious rather than judgemental. If they do have external influences impacting their school life, talk to them about the expectations you have for them within your classroom. You may also have to either engage in a discussion about differences or look at the situation on a wider scale, involve the whole school and pastoral or year leaders, or whatever other across the whole school system the school has.

Self-esteem

Low self-esteem causes a misplaced attitude towards others. Enviousness of others can cause name calling in a derogatory fashion so as to bring the other person down. This can become very debilitating as the thing they often name call is actually something they wish they could recognise in themselves. They call a person a swot, for example, when they themselves may be wishing that they were more intelligent.

Strategy

Discuss with the person their attitude to others in an enquiring way, to ascertain any possible motive that may indicate envy or dissatisfaction with themselves. Lead the questioning to help them recognise that being rude about others does nothing to uplift themselves. Then explore things that could help them to help themselves. It is sad that those who have found school life easy and the academic challenges enjoyable are often on the receiving end of name calling. This can often be because they are perceived as siding with adults and the school system, when those calling them names are struggling with both those things. Your conversation may need to strengthen the resolve of the victim at the same time as speaking to and challenging the perpetrator.

Possible challenges to sense of coherence

Model

Name calling is often a negative protective action used as self-defence; attack is often seen as the best form of defence. Perhaps the person or group of people being insulted can influence change towards the name-caller, which causes concern. They could turn friends away from them for example.

Strategy

Look to see if anything has changed or could change that causes concern, linked to the person they are name calling. Provide reassurance, and when able help them look for alternative ways of managing the change. Friendships change, and sometimes the challenge for children and students is to know how to manage the change. They may also have seen from adults that when a relationship breaks down then it is often followed by vindictive name calling and actions towards each other. You may have to explain that relationships sometimes run their own course and they can look back at what was good and move on, taking good memories with them. They can remain friends still but just not as close, with all that used to entail.

Manageable

As a protective measure, name calling can also be used to deflect from something that they can often feel they are not able to manage. This could be related to a number of things, including looks, ability, friendship group, family situation, academic ability, health …. Or even the work you are setting, as they know you will spend time correcting the name calling and not get on with the lesson.

Strategy

The name calling in itself potentially has its cause in a variety of reasons, as have been highlighted. Talking and asking questions to ascertain why they have targeted the specific person or group of people will help you in finding alternative coping strategies. I have known situations when name calling within schools has begun when the parents of the children involved have fallen out – the effects of what the adults are saying about each other then spill over into the relationships of the children. I am thinking about Romeo and Juliet at the moment and the effects of the animosity of adults on children.

Meaningful

It may be that, before the incident, the person they are attacking had attacked something or someone that is important to their life. Name calling is the easiest and most direct approach to get back at someone and can therefore become very visceral. The insult that involves a person's 'Mum' will generally be a good enough reason for the problem to escalate. The aftermath of this insult can become extreme. For some this attack can become a very powerful and meaningful reason for them to return name calling with a vengeance.

Strategy

If this is the reason, the best way to deal with this is to help the person doing the attacking to find a more constructive way to challenge the behaviour of someone than name calling. Challenge them to live up to the standards that they most admire in the person who is being attacked. 'What is the best thing about your mum?' 'What kinds of things does she do?' 'What kind of person does she want you to be?' And to live their lives accordingly. If their mum happens to also be one who can go on the offensive quickly then you may need to approach those questions along the lines of 'What does your mum say to you when you get into trouble at school?', 'Does she expect you to do right?', 'So how proud would she be if you defended her without getting into trouble?', 'Would you like to learn how to say to someone you don't like what they have said, in a way that gets them thinking and also keeps you out of trouble?' Out of control emotions make smart people do and say very silly things and therefore the need for emotional intelligence is necessary. You may need to talk with the person who they have attacked by name calling and challenge them also about their behaviour to see if they have caused the issue in the first place.

Scenario 3: Lack of motivation

For some children, the enthusiasm to learn that they have when they first go into school is slowly snuffed out as they progress through the years. There can be a number of reasons for this but the one influential factor that must always be taken into account is the enthusiasm of the teacher. I have a teacher friend who has just started working in Switzerland. One of the children's parents met with her and asked her what she had done with his son, as a few weeks before she had arrived the son had asked to stop learning French, as he hated it, but now he was asking if he could continue to stay in the lesson as he now loves it! My teacher friend (Manu), has developed her emotional intelligent skills over years of teaching, commented that first and foremost she had made the lessons fun as well as engaging and she had built up a good relationship with all the students in the class. This is all she had done, but as you can see it's enough to change the attitude around completely. If this strategy isn't successful then here are a few other points to consider.

Possible social and emotional causes

Age

Motivation to try things, especially in Key Stages 1 and 2, when students are encouraged by those they respect, is very strong so lack of motivation may well have some emotional or health issues attached to it.

This can lose its attraction as they grow older (ages 8+) and need the motivation from within to continue trying things, at a time when they want to move away from listening and following adults. A lack of motivation can signal a variety of possible causes. At this age and through adolescence, brain maturation as well as other body changes require the body to have significant amounts of calories and sleep to manage tasks.

Strategy

Check to see what they have eaten as well as how much sleep they are getting. A lot of young children have to be looked after by various family members who don't always live close to each other, which can often lead to late nights and disrupted sleep. Check with the parents or guardians regarding time away from school to see what pattern they have. As they get older and slightly more independent ask them to write out a sleep and food diary for the past few days to see if they are getting enough of both. This need only take a few moments and can be weaved into some lessons. It will also be a good conversation starter with their friends and provide you with an overview of habits. If food is an issue, i.e. no breakfast, then perhaps the school can provide breakfast or free lunches? Teach the whole class about the needs of the body during the period of both brain and body maturation and growth in regard to sleep and food. Explain to them that this can be linked to their own performance, and their ability to try and to concentrate. It may also, for some, be the first sign that an eating disorder may be present. This is also a good time to check on sleep and the use of social media. I believe the pressure that young people feel to stay in contact with each other and to continually seek the affirmation from their peers that they are included and liked, is a powerful influence, leading to the loss of all-important sleep.

Home/personal life

Lack of motivation can signify that the person's life may have some negative input, which takes away the desire for them to improve. Health and personal issues may be the cause, along with personal lifestyle choices which may be affecting the intrinsic motivation for an individual. If those who *should* be providing them with nurture and love have a negative effect on their lives, this can lead to a lack of motivation. The lack of praise and recognition for achievement can also be a factor.

Strategy

Lack of motivation can often be linked to detrimental external influences so it's important to know the person you are dealing with as much as possible. Try to find out as much as you can about their lives that might hint at a possible reason for this most basic life skill to be switched off. Often it will be associated with emotional or psychological issues so the questions may highlight facts that need referring to your designated safeguard person. Ask the student what they think the effect would be if you were to phone home and say to … (at this point ask them who they think would be the main contact at home) what a good person you are, what would they say? If the student gives a positive response, then you can build upon what they think the response would be and say that you will indeed be calling home and we will see how we can also keep developing such good feedback from you. If the answer is negative, then ask what they think it would be that their contact person would be impressed with? You may have to reiterate how impressed you are with them, remembering it's important to praise the person for who they are socially and emotionally as well as for any academic or other work they produce.

Relationship/belonging

Lack of belonging and/or positive relationships will often affect the focus of a person's life, as well as sometimes leading to their questioning of the reasons for trying: 'If I am not liked, why should I try?' The sad consequence about rejection is that the person facing rejection becomes by their very actions less likeable. They often become surly, de-motivated, angry and negative – which adds to a spiral that is hard to escape from.

Strategy

Check the person's relationship with people within the school, class or tutor group to see how they fit in. One person can also affect the motivation of others, so check if they are being influenced by others to not try. Often this can be superseded by having a better relationship with you as the teacher, and you can become an external motivating factor until they gain confidence to be motivated by themselves. Look to see what you can say and do which others can see, that shows that you have an interest in them and like them. Talk to them outside of class when you see them and make a point of smiling at them and being pleased to see them. They are having to work through a lot of negativity, and the light from your face and smile can help them move from the dark place.

Self-esteem

To have the attitude to try something new requires the ability to cope when things don't go as planned. This requires a level of confidence, therefore lack of trying can often be associated with the fear of failure.

Strategy

The belief that you have in them as a person can often be the influencing factor in raising their own self-esteem and to try something new as they will recognise that even failure has not affected your belief in them. The phrase 'Even better if …', can have a debilitating effect on some who tend to always feel whatever they do is never good enough; whereas what they have just done is often as good as it can be at the time and should be celebrated. Telling someone they can do something once they have told you they can't tends to encourage the person to really show you that they can't as you don't believe them, so they try even less. If this happens, help the student to recognise your excellence as a teacher and they will be able to do even more than they think, with your help, as you are amazing!

Possible challenges to sense of coherence

Model

Trying something new or persisting with something when it requires resilience often requires stability within the rest of life so as to be able to focus and achieve most effectively. Too much change or too many challenges can cause overload and therefore a reluctance to try or do anything else.

Strategy

Make sure that your lessons and interactions with the person are very consistent. This includes how you praise and encourage them. Use measured forms which are consistent with the amount of effort used. Too much praise when they have only done a small thing is mis-matched and leaves very little room for higher praise when merited. Check also if changes are going on outside of school with friends and family. If family members are ill or may be experiencing challenging events, this can often find its way into the minds of the children so discreetly ask if things are OK outside of school with the family. 'Is everyone OK?' I have been informed about cancer being diagnosed within the family, someone going into prison, someone coming out of prison, grandparent's death, eviction. Any of these events in a young person's mind can make the most interesting of lessons irrelevant.

Manageable

It could be as simple as what is being asked of them is too hard and comes from a belief that it's impossible to do. Differentiation is especially key for a lot of lessons when one size won't fit all.

Strategy

Check to see their understanding of what is being asked of them: Is it too difficult? Or too easy? Often peer assistance is a great way to motivate some who can't try, as they tend to listen to and work with someone their own age showing them what to do and helping them.

This has the added benefit of helping them feel more of a sense of belonging. Also, if you know someone slightly older who also struggled with the same thing but overcame it, see if they wouldn't mind spending 15 minutes after school or during a lunch break explaining it to the student who is having difficulty. You will be surprised at the amount of people who don't mind helping others. It's a win–win on a lot of fronts and self-esteem, social and emotional competence are also improved.

Meaningful

Quite simply, if what is being asked of them has no meaning or purpose related to their life, then this is automatically followed by a lack of motivation to try or be involved. The student may have said to you, 'What's the point?' and on a lot of levels they do have a point. It is just because someone has decided that that is what they need to learn. Providing them with this as an answer will only further embed their belief that learning is a waste of time.

Strategy

To engage in anything constructively, it has to be meaningful and meet the personal needs and values of an individual. Ask them, do they see the point in what they are being asked to do? Be ready for an honest answer. Also remember that what is meaningful and relevant for you may have no meaning for them so trying to convince them of your reasoning is not an option. Remember that their age may limit their answer, as they are really only interested in the here and now, in this minute of their lives. They are not thinking ahead to work, university, exams, they are only thinking 'Why should I bother this very minute to engage my brain?' They may be reasoning that they don't need the skill, or the knowledge, thinking that they may not even be taking the subject next year so it's not important. Helping them to move on from this way of thinking may just boil down to the fact that you can become the very reason the task becomes meaningful just by being the one who asks them to do it and engage in it. This requires you being important to them and making sure you are relevant and understand their lives. It will also mean that the lesson will have to be fun and engaging on all levels for them. It would take a lot of emotional maturity to actively engage in something that seems pointless and irrelevant, as well as being dry and boring.

Scenario 4: Difficulty concentrating on one task for a length of time

The attention span of individuals is changing. Think for yourself about the amount of time you spend reading an article on a web page, or how hard it is having to focus for any length of time on one topic. I have heard CEOs of Academies suggest that lessons should be 90 minutes long, not for the reason that it makes the lesson more focused but simply because teachers having to deliver those lessons cannot wing it for that length of time, so it makes them work better! The length of a lesson is never the issue; as long as the lesson is engaging, stimulating and challenging then the children and students will be learning. The lesson, whatever its length, needs to involve constant changes. Change is often as good as a rest for the mind so think about short stimulating activities that build upon each other. The length of time those items should be is outlined below. For students and children to stay focused involves a higher functional aspect of their brain and this will come with training and age. I have not yet seen it develop with detentions, warnings, or simply being told to do so.

Possible social and emotional causes

Age

Children aged five to six-years-old typically can attend to one activity that is of interest to them for around 10 to 15 minutes at a time and should generally be able to filter out small distractions. According to Kids Growth, the attention span of a child or teen who is actively trying to pay attention is 3 to 5 minutes for every year of the child's age. As a result, a 13-year-old has an attention span between 39 and 65 minutes, while a 16-year-old is capable of paying attention for 48 to 80 minutes. It has to be remembered that this attention span applies to things they are interested in.

Strategy

Activities such as spending more time outdoors, exercise, cognitive training, and meditation are ways in which people at any age can enhance their ability to concentrate. The brain can develop better concentration skills and encouraging this growth is never a waste of time. Cognitive games such as 'Simon Says' and 'I went to the shop and I bought ... ' can improve concentration levels, especially for children with ADHD. If you use games, then explain first to the whole class the reasoning behind the game and what you are aiming to achieve and why. You can make the game relevant of course to what you are needing to teach. You can use the 'I went to the shops and I bought ...' structure and change it to 'I came to the lesson and I learnt about ...'. Then require them to remember one item that they learnt or a new thing they have tried. See how many everyone can remember from each other. You can also include 'I came to the lesson and I was impressed with ... Ryan because he helped me ... '.

Home/personal life

There are many external factors that can influence the ability to concentrate, including lack of sleep, lack of food, over-consumption of energy drinks, relationship issues, stress, drugs, emotional upset. Just for your own research, ask your class how many of them are using social media after midnight? It is an ever-growing habit among teenagers and will inevitably have an effect on them during the next day.

Strategy

Check to see what is going on in the person's life externally as well as what they have eaten and drunk before the lesson. Ask about sleep, gaming and phone use at night. The issues that you might uncover may require the school's intervention as well as contact with parents or carers. Just as preparing for a sporting event requires meticulous dietary preparation as well as training, rest and practice, help them to realise that to get the best from school and the lessons requires similar focus to get the desired reward.

Relationship/belonging

Relationships can massively impact a person's ability to concentrate. Not being part of the classroom as well as not having a good relationship with the teacher can result in lack of engagement to what is going on within the class. Imagine the effect of trying to work with others who you knew didn't like you or didn't include you, and how that knowledge would invade your thoughts constantly during the time together. This is even more keenly felt by those who are looking for a sense of belonging with their peers during their school years.

Strategy

If they don't have any friends within the class, seek to establish a good working relationship with them to improve their sense of belonging first and foremost with you and be their support during the early stages. Comment about how well they can maintain their concentration and set small targets for them to complete before you return. Agree beforehand with them what that target is going to be. If they do have friends, these students can often be enlisted into helping them stay focused, by working together on specific tasks. Always explain what you are trying to do, for example, helping them develop concentration skills. Have them agree they are willing to do that and make sure that the person who is trying to improve their concentration also agrees to help them. Monitor this closely to start with so that they have small victories and then build upon that over time. Thank them at the end of the lesson as well as reminding them of the strategy at the start of the lesson. If they work together in other lessons, then see if they can also employ the same strategy there as well.

Self-esteem

A lack of belief in themselves in the ability to concentrate can often become a self-fulfilling prophesy, especially if they have been told off in the past for their lack of concentration. Negativity in oneself is debilitating on so many levels and this is the first item that will need to be addressed so be aware of how you have tried to encourage students. Warnings of detention or the threat that the student will have to return to complete the work 'in their own time' are poor motivating tools and should be avoided. Very rarely will you have a student recognising that a detention is a positive motivating factor for change. It is a factor and for some an influencer for change, as they want to avoid spoiling their own time, so it has to become meaningful for it to work. Yet there are far more beneficial helpful motivating factors for you to use that will improve the person's own ability as well as maintain a positive working relationship with you.

Strategy

Check to see if they have difficulty in other lessons and assure them that you are there to help improve their concentration. Explain that each week as they grow and mature, they will have more ability. Encourage them with the thought that they can improve and end the problem of being told off if you work together on it.

Possible challenges to sense of coherence

Model

The habit of only concentrating for short periods may have become the model they are used to. The attention span in young people is dropping, and the idea of having to do something which they have no experience of success in can cause them to give up.

Strategy

As concentration is a developmental skill, explain that through the year with you it will be something that you will be seeking to develop. Highlight the need for it throughout life and that this will require mental hard work. Assure them that there will be breaks, so that concentrating does not become a task they dread. At the start of the year you can ask them about their ability to concentrate so as to work during the early stages at their optimum. You can also ask them what they think they should do if they find themselves getting distracted. Have them also write down the length of time they can concentrate in their book and use that as the starting point to build upon. Have lessons when you are only going to see how the length of time has increased so they know they are going to have to focus. Make the need to concentrate part of the model of your lessons.

Manageable

Is what they are being asked to concentrate upon within their level of ability or is it below their level of ability? Both of these will impact their desire to focus.

Strategy

Check the person's level of understanding, compare their ability to what they are being asked to do and set the concentration level appropriate to their age as well as to their ability. Remind them that you are there to help and develop the skill. Using an aid to help them stay focused for a length of time could help, such as egg timers of various lengths as well as countdown clocks and pieces of music that last for specific lengths of time. If you are going to use music, then keep it instrumental. I always like to use classical music. Mozart is a favourite of mine. It's a good way to introduce unfamiliar music to them. Explain this piece of music will last (for a number of minutes) and then say this is how long you will have to complete the task. If you say that this is going to be tricky and requires maturity and focus and not many people are able to manage this at your age, they will be delighted to show you that they can!

Meaningful

Is what they are being asked to do meaningful? Teenagers and young people tend to live for the immediate and having to concentrate on something in which they find no meaning relevant for their lives will become a waste of their time. It is always going to be meaningful to chat with their friends, relax, do nothing and see if they can make it through the lesson without doing much. We have an in-built desire to gossip and relax. If you don't believe me see how long you enjoy doing a task and how often you become tired and hope you don't have to do it again? It is a normal hard-wired experience as we will always prefer to be saving energy and involved in social engagement – it's what we as a species specialise in, so your lessons will always have to compete with this natural desire.

Strategy

Find out if they understand why they are doing what you are asking. Make the answer relevant to their lives *now* as much as possible. Explain that the skill of concentrating on a subject carries far more benefit for life than perhaps the task they are doing. Help them to understand that this is a life skill mixed into the lesson. Try to employ, as much as you can, the elements of discussion at the start of the lesson to help you build a platform on which to build the learning. Have a time limit for the discussion so that they know it will be coming to an end. Discussions can often become very stimulating and engaging, and unless you can manage to weave it into a productive conclusion a discussion can easily over-run, and will simply eat into your time.

Scenario 5: Chatting continually

Possible social and emotional causes

If you ask children and students 'What is the most important thing about school?', the answer is often meeting with friends. For some, school is a social club with annoying adults running around trying to stop them chatting with their friends. It is lovely that they are chatting and socially engaging without the use of a mobile phone, yet we know that this can become an issue when we need them to focus and learn. Always check if the chatting is relevant to the learning taking place. I often overhear chatting and upon investigation it is one friend either helping another or offering an explanation and providing further information and understanding to their friend. So, check before asking for quiet again. Sometimes the level of explaining being given is worthy of the whole class hearing.

How you manage the low level chatting that is off task, whilst still enabling them to engage in a positive and rewarding activity, will have a lot to do with how confident you are that you can bring them back on task and desist from their chat, as well as how much work is being done to add to their learning. For those who require a little more prompting here are a few things to bear in mind.

Age

Good communication skills are vital for the social and emotional development of young people. The need for young people of all ages to talk about their feelings, ideas, issues and thoughts is central to how they build friendships and establish their place in the world. It is hard to regulate this within a classroom where ideas and thoughts are meant to flow, especially after a holiday or weekends when friends want to re-connect, or even after a lunch break where the topic of conversation was in their eyes very important. Their need to have positive affirmation is met by speaking and interacting with each other.

Strategy

Add listening skills and social etiquette to the learning requirements for them all, along with the educational expectations, before it becomes an issue. Ask them where else could they use this skill? Set tasks for them to talk about and share, and also talk to them about the best way you can use to get them to listen. Ask them what other teachers do to get them to listen and stop talking and ask which strategy they like and adopt that. I have had children and students say to me that others shout and it's ok if I do that as then it helps them stop. I point out to them that I like to use strategies that work with adults as well as children and I am not too sure adults would appreciate being shouted at so what else can we try?

Inform them that they have just a couple of minutes upon arrival to listen and respond to each other whilst everyone settles and then you will start the lesson. Explain this is no different to how a meeting starts within business as everyone gathers together to discuss the agenda and the adults know they need to be quick as the meeting needs to start. Time spent explaining what you want, the reason you want it, and why it is going to be beneficial for them as well as you, is never wasted. I see too many teachers spending time trying to get the class to be quiet when a short time explaining classroom etiquette would achieve the required end. Give it a go!

Home/personal life

The environment within the home and with friends can often be a learning place for social skills, such as listening and not interrupting others. Waiting in turn to speak is often only taught within the classroom and has no bearing upon everyday experiences outside of the classroom. They also get used to speaking loudly and over each other, and this for some is a social norm. Being quiet and working is often again for some a new experience, as when they are at home, they may have to contend with ordinary background noise from family, television, music and other siblings. For some, listening to music at the same time as doing their homework is the norm so they are used to coping and working with distractions – for them, a quiet classroom environment is in itself very strange.

Strategy

Find out about what they do within their own social time. Make the session a whole class session to explore the length of time they need to be quiet for them to focus on one topic. This lesson lends itself to so many different subjects, for example: in maths, measure the percentage of time spent being quiet; in history, explore what happened to those who spoke when they shouldn't; and in English, write about the rewards of being quiet and listening to others. Make the idea of listening meaningful for them. We all like to be listened to, hence the need to speak over others so we get heard. As you listen to them and allow them to speak, they will also get used to the idea of taking it in turns. Leading by example is always a powerful tool. Shouting for quiet teaches them this is the norm and they readily adopt it themselves. Highlight to them the inability of our brain to listen to things as well as really focus. We can do both on a simple level but if it's something that requires our attention we can't concentrate and speak and listen at the same time. How often do they put music or a film on pause if they have to speak to their friend on the phone? Or if they keep it on in the background do they tend to have to rewind to make sure they haven't missed anything? Highlight the fact that you don't have a pause or rewind button in the class.

Relationship/belonging

Sharing thoughts and stating one's own ideas and preferences are often a good way to cement friendships and through children's lives the need for reassurance and a sense of belonging is very strong. This can often overrule the social niceties of the classroom and what the teacher is saying. Adults find it hard to repress the thoughts and not speak when with friends in different events when silence is sought, so imagine how much harder this is for the immature young person.

Strategy

Chatty people often need people to listen to them and answer because they think it's rude not to, which causes more problems. Talk to all those involved to find a strategy they can start to use that will prevent others talking and answering for the good of the whole class. Explain that this is an alternative to sanctions or consequences. Understand that this will take time to embed, but as long as they try it will get better. Explain the benefits of friends working together for the good of each other. Speak to the class about being a friend that helps the one chatting to stay quiet, in order for them to learn to concentrate. Enlist the friends to be the ones to police each other and restrict the chat amongst themselves. Chatting is their issue and they need to learn to manage themselves. It is a skill that should be transferable around all lessons and if they do develop good listening skills, highlight how respectful it makes them towards you and seek to encourage them to do so in all lessons, so your colleagues can experience the same respect.

Self-esteem

Confirmation of their standing within the class or with the teacher can often result in speaking out. Being noticed and feeling important helps some to raise their own self-esteem, which again outweighs the problem of being told off.

Strategy

Build a good relationship with the people chatting and demonstrate the skill of listening to them, modelling the behaviour you wish to see from them. Explain what you are doing and that you would like their cooperation to make things work. Aim to build them up by highlighting their mature respectful attitude. When a time comes when you think they are likely to start chatting and take over the lesson with their chatting then pre-empt it by letting them know that in a minute you will be having a discussion and you will require them to listen and be quiet for the first part and only when you say their name and ask for their opinion will you want them to say something. If they have something very important to say and find it hard to stay quiet, then they can write it down on a piece of paper and wait to be asked to share. Make sure that you remember to ask them as well as commend them for controlling themselves later in the lesson.

Possible challenges to sense of coherence

Model

Chatting can be a way of coping with stress. This could be brought on by any change that is being dealt with, e.g. in the topic being studied, in friendship groups, in the classroom itself, or perhaps issues with their family. Trying to take their mind off things that they don't like or having to think about things which rekindle something they are trying to avoid can become a reason for some as to why they chat a lot. Sometimes the weather triggers chatting. You will notice that if it's very windy outside then it enlivens people; snow, lightning etc. all add to the excitement. There's not a lot you can do about the weather but at least you can be aware it may be the cause of what you are having to deal with if chatting is something that is not typical with some of the children and students.

Strategy

Find out if any changes are going on within their lives that may be causing anxiety. If it is a change of class, or a new topic, or even you being a new teacher, allow a few moments of calming down time before reminding them of expected behaviour in a relaxed tone, that brings them back on task. If it is the weather then listen to what they are saying about the snow or lightning, or how they nearly got blown over, and then after a few moments let them see they need to calm down as we all have some work to do. Your calmness in tone and approach will help in calming them down.

Manageable

Some people are by their very nature chatty. You know those who always talk in meetings and have something to say in the adult world. They engage their tongue before the brain has a chance to stop it. They also may just find it very hard to be quiet and no one has helped them develop techniques to do that. The chances are that when asked they will explain that they have tried but just can't keep it up. They may often need an external reminder to help them.

Strategy

For those who are more extrovert in their approach to life, help them to develop methods to help control themselves. Hand them five lolly sticks and only let them speak five times during a lesson – each time they speak they have to hand over one stick. Use your proximity to remind them that they need to try to stay quiet. Warn them before the others about the need to listen so they have time to control themselves. Devise a strategy with them that acts as a reminder. Often students and children like to have a report card, which they then have to hand in to the teacher so as to remind them of what they are trying to achieve. This is often because they have been struggling with different aspects of classroom etiquette. These cards do have their uses and for some it is the consistent reminder that they need. If it is used as a positive enforcer for them, that's fine. But if it becomes a focus on the fact that they haven't managed to do what has been asked, it becomes an issue as the extenuating circumstances are seldom if ever looked at. The student then often feels worse as they have in their own eyes failed again.

Meaningful

Anything that requires change must first be meaningful, and punishment is not the best method to persuade a person that being quiet has now become meaningful. One of the important things to bear in mind is that chatting is important them, and shouting out is who they are, and therefore this is the more meaningful aspect of their behaviour that you have to help them to master. Resolving this issue starts with you getting to know them and talking with them to see what you can use as a strategy to help them.

Strategy

Highlight the benefits of listening and controlling themselves – this is a simple introduction to the reason they should be trying to control themselves. Help them to realise that the approach is a sign of maturity and respect. One of the hardest issues they often have to overcome is the need they have to tell you something that is meaningful for them right now! They think you will be interested in their issue, and it's important to them that you hear it regardless of what they know they should be doing. It will disturb the lesson, but they don't care as it's so important. Let them know they can tell you once the lesson has finished, explaining that you are genuinely interested and can't wait to hear, but now is not the time. Please smile and show genuine interest when saying this, to help them realise your honesty in the matter. Make sure you do follow up on this!

Scenario 6: Breaking basic rules to do with dress code: Do your tie up, tuck your shirt in

Possible social and emotional causes

Once early adolescence kicks in we know that children like to break free from the adult management of their lives. This is strengthened as they become teenagers, so the basic rules that schools adopt can become an easy target for them to butt up against and see what they can get away with to highlight their independence. This is also a time when uniform fashions take on a life of their own – ties get tied in a specific way that is away from the norm, shirts inevitably get left untucked, and whatever the children or students choose to adopt becomes the norm as long as it differs from what convention dictates it should be. This flaunting of the rules in some way is to be expected and understanding this should help us not to become emotional and annoyed when it happens. Our approach should be to look more into the reason why they wish to do so and help them learn through this period of their lives how they can find individuality without breaking rules and getting into trouble. Here are a few things to consider.

Age

From the age of five, children like to be included in the discussion regarding the setting of rules. Aged eight and upwards, they begin challenging rules they see as unfair, and this continues through teenage years. Aged 15 onwards, a greater understanding of the implications of rule breaking starts to emerge, along with a better approach to the reasons for following rules.

Strategy

Within your classroom establish a strong classroom etiquette and emphasise the reasons for following it. Always highlight social expectations and norms. School is a place to learn about life not just for education. The secondary school setting will always be the place for teenagers to test the resolve of schools to adhere to their own rules. Consistency is key as it won't take long for either the class etiquette to be recognised as something they should follow, or something they can get away with ignoring. Be consistent with your expectations and comments as well as with your praise. Explain that your room as well as your area is important to you and that means you care about everything about them as a person you are there to develop.

Home/personal life

Following rules starts at home, and primary school children especially are influenced by the approach of those who are looking after them. As mentioned, secondary school children see rules as more of an area to test their own individuality upon and can find it hard to conform to rules set by others.

Strategy

Establish links with parents as soon as you can; waiting until things go wrong is too late. This will help in so many areas and it will also give you an insight as to the expectations of parents regarding dress sense and conformity. If personal and home life are not very good you may need to be the one who offers the extra emotional support and encouragement to get the basics right. If you find you are having to mention more than three times the tie or shirt then have a more in-depth conversation to find out what lies behind the refusal. Often there can be financial reasons as to why things become a problem regarding clothing. I have known children and students who have had to live in two or sometimes three different houses and washing and managing of clothes can become an issue. Unfortunately, it is not unusual for some children to have to live in temporary accommodation and this will also have an impact upon how they view themselves and how tidy they normally are. Be sensitive in your discussions and adherence to the school's expectations.

Relationship/belonging

Secondary school and the influence of peer pressure can often be a stronger pull to conform than the school or the teacher. Sloppy dressing is one way to show annoyance and lack of belonging towards the school that is 'forcing them' to wear it.

Strategy

Wearing a uniform correctly and with pride often needs to be linked to a sense of belonging to the school and what the school stands for. If this isn't established, then the sense of belonging to you and the influence that you have will have to compete with peer pressure. Get to know them as much as you can. Dealing with a group of similar aged people who have the same issue all at once is often a more productive way of dealing with any issue. Look to resolve the situation through them choosing to conform, rather than by threating consequences if they don't.

Self-esteem

Low self-esteem can often lead to poor personal care. Feelings of alienation from the school and the ability to perform well can also result in them not wanting to wear the uniform properly – it just reminds them of the place they don't want to be at.

Strategy

Get to know them and what is going on in their mind. The clothing is a very good indicator of their thoughts and attitude to themselves, to life and to the school itself as well as their home life. Build them up in whatever area they highlight. We know that people generally feel better if they look good and feel clean and tidy, but their life situation may not be conducive for this to happen, so again your sensitivity about the matter will be key for helping them come up with a plan to improve things. It might also be an opportunity for the school to help. I know of many schools that take in school uniforms and wash them for students as it's not possible in their everyday family life for this to happen.

Possible challenges to sense of coherence

Model

People tend to re-do what they have always done, so for some this might mean the way they dress and prepare for school each day. This applies to adults as well and I often wonder about the time spent in preparation for going out and what kind of impression they are wishing to make or even if they have thought about it at all?

Strategy

Ask them what do they think when they put on the school uniform? What do clothes mean to them? What clothes do they like wearing and why? Check out the amount of time they take to get ready and link this to how much time they think it takes to make an impression. Being prepared to develop and grow as a person starts from the moment you get up and choose the attitude for the day. Help build a model of positivity for them. Change the model they have.

Manageable

Some children, as mentioned above, now have more than one address because of personal circumstances, so clothing is not often washed, sorted or available, and that makes the appearance untidy. We have a responsibility to understand the financial as well as the domestic implications of requests we make as a school.

Strategy

Find out about personal circumstances; this might highlight something that the school can assist with. I have seen the attitude of individuals change completely by the addition of a new uniform, purchased by the school when family situations were dire.

Meaningful

All rules should carry meaning and relevance to those that they affect. This is particularly important when affecting the lives of young people in secondary school. The uniform is particularly contentious for some and often can be used as a form of rebellion to see what they can get away with regarding how to wear it.

Strategy

For individuals and groups who persistently flout the expectations regarding uniform it's important to re-establish what is acceptable. Whole school enforcement with buy-in from parents is a must from the start. Highlight the reason that is meaningful for them to follow these rules as a start to them focusing on the fact that this is a school day and social norms are expected when in school. Be clear on what is acceptable, and my advice is always to include equipment as part of the uniform. The expectation is that they come equipped to learn, and this will mean having a pen and other basic equipment to start with. I believe this is an important part of them building a sense of belonging to a school – the school signifies a place of academic learning, which necessitates basic equipment. If you need to hand out pens and other items that they should have brought, this again might have implications related to home life and the school should examine ways with the students to overcome any external problems. Doing so will also show to the children and students that you care for them and want them to fully integrate into what the school has to offer.

Scenario 7: Getting a class to listen to instructions

This is one area in which I see so many different strategies used, and these often end up creating an environment for the rest of the lesson which is not conducive to good relationships. Shouting, ordering, issuing warnings, using a 3-2-1 countdown for them to stop speaking on 1, standing waiting for everyone to be quiet, shushing, calling out specific people's names and telling them to be quiet, lumping them all in together and saying, for example, 'Class 4 be quiet!' or 'Year 9 be quiet!' All of the above tend to be the teacher managing the class and the students and often it's not until a threat of a sanction is issued that classes start to bring themselves into order.

The atmosphere created at the start of the lesson should be one that will then flow through the rest of your time together. I often wonder what response I would get if, when delivering training in schools, I adopted the same techniques to establish quiet as I see and hear teachers using. There are many reasons as to why children and students chat upon arrival and why they take time to bring themselves to order but the overriding point to remember is we are trying to teach them to manage themselves. Your composure and confidence should be evident from the start as you then engage the students. Here are a few points to consider if you encounter problems when starting the lesson and requiring attention from the whole class.

Possible social and emotional causes

Age

At Key Stage 1, school children are keen to explore, talk, move about and try lots of new things and it goes against their natural instincts to sit still and listen. As they move into KS2 they will have understood the expectations placed upon them to listen but will still be easily distracted. At KS3, distraction along with the fear of appearing rude to their friends by stopping talking with them to listen to you is more of an issue. At KS4 they now have the mental competence as well as the understanding of what is expected of them to overcome distractions so as to focus upon you.

Strategy

At KS1, introduce a triangle or small bell to them and explain that you wish them to 'Stand like statues' when they hear it. Then introduce to them simple expectations, possibly linked to videos or music, to lead them on to the next activity (such as tidy up time, sit on the mat time), and have them move into the next activity quietly. At KS2, link the sounds again to commands but introduce table monitors each day to take the lead to help you with gaining quiet in the classroom. Make sure everyone over time has a go at being a monitor, so as to build up the skill of responsibility linked to classroom expectations. At KS3, during your introduction ask them the best way to gain quiet and what you should do if it's not happening. Place the onus upon them to control themselves. Talk about the fear of being rude to their friends when they are talking with them and how they can collectively overcome it so as not to delay the start of the lesson. I am always keen for those who teach music to use a baton and tap the desk just as a conductor does to bring them all into order before the start of any concert. Find out what method is appropriate for the class that is acceptable for all. If you are wishing to use a countdown system to bring a class to order (and this can be introduced with any year group), then it is important to explain the reason as to why it is being introduced, and what your expectations are regarding how to use it. So, for example, you might explain that 'Five' means: pay attention to me; 'Four': stop talking; 'Three': put your pens down and stop what you're doing; 'Two': be prepared to listen; and 'One' means: time for me to start to talk to you. Remember to start your talk with a 'thank you'.

During the lesson you can ask various students what the numbers mean, to check understanding and preparedness for engagement for when you use it. Time spent doing this will reward you in the long run.

Home/personal life

Individuals who find it harder to be quiet may well be growing up in a household full of noise and distractions and the only way to be heard is to be noisy themselves. Others may be more extroverted by nature and therefore their nature is to be speaking, making noise or preferring to have noise around them. I spoke with one child who explained to me that his three brothers all had ADHD and the only way he can be heard is to be louder than them.

Strategy

If there are a few that tend to be noisy and find it hard to be quiet like the rest, find out about their home life and ask when are they quiet? Help them see that you are aiming to help them to learn a social skill and avoid sanctions. Statistically you will have nearly 50% of students who are more extroverts than introverts so ask them how they are going to master the skill of their own personality type. Any answers they give you will help them with becoming more aware and responsible for their actions which they and you can build upon. At KS3 the conversation may need to be more serious; the pull of distraction is very strong as they also seek to impress both their friends and others in the class. Remind them that school and classroom respect are for the benefit of all and their participation is expected. You will also have to do a quick check to be sure that it is meaningful for them to listen at this point as well, which may involve more in-depth time spent with them. Consistency and repetition are key. Keep empathising, in a calm way, it's their problem and they have to learn to master a skill that others have already learnt. Explain that you are going to be reminding them and working with them to find an appropriate method.

Relationship/belonging

Talking over people or refusing to listen often shows a lack of respect and also highlights a lack of relationship with those they are being asked to listen to.

Strategy

Check on your relationship with those who disrupt and refuse to be quiet when you wish the class to do so. Ask them to explain to you their thoughts when the rest of the class is listening, and they choose not to, what are they thinking about at that time, what is it they are wanting to achieve? Ask them what they think of the class and the lesson as a whole, as the talking may be a way of not having to engage. Sometimes the very conversation may help them rethink what has become a habit.

Self-esteem

Lessons are often a place where academic competence and ability is on show and for some this can affect their own self-esteem positively as well as negatively. Any distraction and avoidance will be a blessing for some. In the past, it may have been the reason for them to be excluded from lessons, which has meant them falling behind their peers in a variety of skills. I met a 15-year-old who was unable to read and write, which meant their involvement in any lesson was extremely limited and debilitating for them, leading to them becoming disruptive and especially reluctant to listen to instructions.

Strategy

Check on their overall attitude towards the subject you are teaching; try to find out if it does impact negatively upon their self-esteem because of what it highlights about them. Lessons are about character as well as subject, so you may need to talk about building their character regarding a subject they find difficult.

Possible challenges to sense of coherence

Model

Any disruption to the normal expectations will tend to cause the extrovert types to talk and demonstrate their anxiety and uncertainty.

Strategy

Be consistent in your method and approach towards quiet in the lesson. Take into account age and experience, and model what you expect as well as providing them with the chance to demonstrate their competence. Your proximity to them, and a gentle reminder that in a few moments you are going to call the class to listen so be ready for it, will help them.

Manageable

For some, to be quiet and listen for any length of time will be hard. The ability to stay focused without outside assistance or reminders is a skill that can develop over time. For some it is a skill they haven't learnt to manage.

Strategy

For a disruptive class, keep your need for them to be quiet short to start with and highlight that you will be building it up over time. Give them specific times regarding your input so they learn to manage it. Take short breaks when folks can talk and then return to being quiet. Inform them at all times what it is that you are working towards and why. Have those who find it hard to be quiet sit nearer you or move to stand near them as you address the class. For younger children it is very important to emphasise that you will not answer any questions or make a comment to them whilst you are talking to the whole class. It is very easy to fall into the trap of answering simple quick questions from children and thinking that you have dealt with the issue. However, for a young mind, what registers is that you have recognised them individually, they have enjoyed the attention and would like it again. Other children will also have seen the attention and want some of it as well, and before you know it you have a lot of little hands up and multiple callings out vying for you to quickly answer their questions.

Meaningful

Being quiet and listening to you will have to be meaningful. This includes both being meaningful to their own set of values and expectations as to their own behaviour, and meaningful because they have a relationship with you and/or what it is that you are talking about.

Strategy

Is what you are wanting to say to them meaningful? It is very important that your input is relevant to them at the very moment you are speaking. 'Why should I listen to you now?' You should question if your input is necessary and if it is important to the lesson for them to pay attention, then you can explain to them why. Be careful to make sure that the input is important for them as well as you for them to listen to, as it can often happen that the focus is important in the mind of the teacher only.

Scenario 8: Students who find it hard to cope with the stress of exams

Stress and anxiety are going to become common words that you will encounter within your time at school. These conditions will affect the staff as well as children and students, and often peak during times of assessments and exams so can be a relevant issue for both primary and secondary schools. I tend to avoid the over used expression of exam stress and talk about ordinary feelings of anxiety when dealing with something that has meaning and importance. For those in primary I recommend making whatever assessment the children have to go through as normal and as everyday as possible. The unfortunate attitude of many adults stressing the importance of a result upon a child has led to the rise of unnecessary anxiety in children and you can be the person of reason and calm for those you are teaching as well as to the parents.

For those in secondary school highlight the normality of the emotions they are experiencing and the need for them to find their own solution through the variety of advice on offer to learn how to manage the emotions. They will never be free from normal everyday pressures in their lives as they enter the adult world, and this is as good a time as any to recognise the fact and learn to deal with it. They can be encouraged to think where the pressure is coming from – is it the fear of the result, their parents, their peers, their lack of preparedness? When they can pinpoint it, you can help them start to look for solutions to manage it. If they can't because it's out of their control, then help them to start to accept they have to manage only what they can influence.

You can also help them examine what would they wish they could change, looking back at the lead up to this point. Students often say to me that they wish they had studied harder. This can be a great introduction to the usefulness of hindsight and the introduction of two of the best words in the English language: Next time!

Here are a few ideas to bear in mind when the time comes for you to be the person of calm.

Possible social and emotional causes

Age

Students aged 10 or 11, when faced with tests or becoming stressed, tend to lose the capacity for logic and abstract thinking. This means they will likely find the pressure of exams, with so much importance being placed upon by schools and parents, equally stressful.

Strategy

For younger ones, provide them with time to play and express their childishness as a good outlet from the coming test. They will show various aspects of how the anxiety is affecting them and it's important for you to be aware of this. Expect to see some changes in their behaviour, often in becoming silly and more playful, so having times of play organised will help. Your calm consistency on expectations should always be maintained.

Listen to your tone of voice and stay relaxed when discussing the need for the assessment. Highlight your desire for them to do their best in remembering the things you have taught them, but stress the most important thing you have taught them this year is to be kind, thoughtful and nice to each other and themselves and no matter what they achieve in one assessment their greatest achievement and success in your eyes is all they have done for each other as a class and the pleasure it is for you to have got to know them. You can talk to them all individually through the weeks leading up to the assessment in a one-to-one, and mention what it is you like about them, what aspects of their personality you have noticed and admire over the past year you have taught them. Point out to them the things they can build upon as they grow up that will make them successful first and foremost as a nice human being. You don't need to wait for Year 6 to do this, you can make this part of the end of whatever year you have been teaching and see what effect this has upon the self-esteem of the children.

For the older students, this is for some the first time they are being asked to do something that will be life impacting. Your attitude toward the exams can reduce the stress level. Use words such as exciting rather than important, tricky, hard, long … etc. Encourage them when asked about any upcoming exam to answer by saying 'I am excited about the exam.' You will be surprised what the simple change in the words can have upon attitude.

Home/personal life

Sleep, eating and general social life will play a key role in how well (or not) people can manage the stress of exams. The pressure of friends, relatives, parents, siblings can all impact upon a person's ability to cope. An inability to revise appropriately also causes anxiety for some.

Strategy

Check how much sleep they are getting and what they are eating. 'As an energy-consumer, the brain is the most expensive organ we carry around with us,' says Dr. Marcus Raichle, professor of medicine at Washington University School of Medicine in St. Louis. While the brain represents just 2% of a person's total body weight, it accounts for 20% of the body's energy use.

Lack of food will impact on its ability to function successfully. Lack of sleep will also play a part in concentration. Check to see what the school can do to lessen the impact of poor self-management and revision space. I do like to encourage schools to provide a banana for everyone at the start of the day for any exam that is happening. Make sure that if you are planning on doing this it happens with the mock exams as well.

Relationship/belonging

The feeling of having to face an exam and also feeling isolated and without any sense of belonging in the home, or within school, can massively impact the ability for the person to cope with the stress of the exams. It will also impact the importance of the exams themselves as they cease to have relevance in a person's life if they don't have a sense of belonging with people around them.

Strategy

It is crucial that you act as a personal support to every individual during times of stress and anxiety. Link together people to mutually support, work with and revise, making sure everyone is included. Let them all know of your care and attention and support. Be the stability and calmness they need. For the older students you can become a very important alternative adult in their life, helping provide motivations, hope, care, interest and belief in them which will help them towards their feeling of belonging to someone.

Self-esteem

Exams are an easy way to highlight inadequacies as well competencies and as long as we remain so narrowly restricted to this inadequate method of assessment, we will have those whose self-esteem will be affected by them.

Strategy

The exams by their very limitations are only a narrow indicator of competence. You should endeavour to highlight more that the personal attitude towards doing your best, and the character that is demonstrated in so doing, is by far a better indicator of self-worth. Raise their self-esteem by looking beyond the exams to the person who is maturing before you. This is just as important, in primary schools, for their young lives, as it is in secondary schools as students look to move forward towards their adult life. What kind of character and person are they wishing to become? Well there will never a better time to demonstrate this character than during a time of pressure.

Possible challenges to sense of coherence

Model

This is the least of the problems as the exam date, length and topic to some extent is known. Yet because it is often for some, the first time they are involved in a life impacting situation, then they have no reference point.

Strategy

Doing a dry run in the hall or room or with the assistance they will have before the event will always help. Remember to include the reminder about getting a good night's sleep and breakfast on the day so as to make it more realistic. Review how they felt and what they would change or keep the same relating to the situation not just the answers given in the exam.

I encourage secondary schools, if possible, to offer a variety of environments or areas just before entering into the exam. Some students like to have quiet and contemplation before embarking upon an exam, others like to listen to music privately, others like to do last minute reading, whilst others just want to chat with their friends. Whatever helps them prepare, let them choose so they can arrive as relaxed as possible.

Manageable

As they will have no idea what questions they will get this is the main focus of their anxiety. Over-revising or poor last-minute revising can lead to anxiety, as the brain is unable to shift so much to long term memory which will be helpful for the exam.

Strategy

A very good form of revision is the pair questions with answers game. Make 40 laminated cards: 20 questions, and 20 answers, turned upside down. They have to take it in turns to turn one card over at a time and then turn one more to see if they can match either a question or answer to their first card. The person who gets the most pairs wins. This is a strategy you can encourage them to use throughout their school life and not just necessarily for exam preparation. The more sets of laminated cards that you can encourage the students to make will build up your resources as well. For others, you could devise an orienteering course around the school and each point in the school area represents a specific point they need to remember. They can then mentally walk the school remembering key facts.

Meaningful

Not seeing the point of the exam and not being able to find any relevance to learning a subject they won't use or don't like and then being asked to be tested in it is for some a complete waste of their time and they disengage or give up. Or, conversely, placing so much importance upon an exam that the pressure mounts up leads to worry about failing.

Strategy

For both those scenarios the approach is the same. The exams are a means to an end and character and attitude are being tested much more than academic ability. Whatever the person is seeking to do with their future lives will be impacted by the way they deal with important stressful situations. The brain is making new neural pathways linked to the situation and experience it is faced with. If they choose to give up and not bother just because it's too hard, or they don't see the point, that will be an indication of how they will approach things in their adult life. Encourage them to become the adult they want to be and for some this will mean they ignore the irrelevance of the exam but to do their best regardless and aim for a good result. For those for whom exams are so important, help them also to focus upon the building of their character and attitude in respect to their chosen career. I always stress that the new employer will be more interested in their character and emotional intelligence rather than simply the results of a test. They can work with and develop a good character. These soft skills are the skills of the future.

Another important point to remember is the more they stress the more they start to use the limbic part of their brain, formed from the age of 3 to 8. This is driven far more by their emotions and fight, flight, flock and freeze mentality and less by the higher thinking rational, calm part of the brain that is able to find connections and new ideas. This part of the brain has been developing since the age of 15 and they need to be using it as much as possible. Do they want an 8-year-old's brain taking their exam or a 15/16-year-old! Focus upon their maturity and ability to develop the skills to manage stress and talk with them afterwards about techniques they found useful and will adopt for the next one.

Scenario 9: Students who show a lack of respect for you as a teacher

Put simply, respect is allowing yourself and others to do and be their best, therefore the lack of respect within a school or classroom fights against the very nature of the purpose of a teacher. It is therefore vital for respect to be shown and experienced by all yet unfortunately this is not always the case. The lack of respect shown by some towards caring thoughtful professional teachers and others can have long lasting emotional effect and often leads to some leaving the profession.

Yet the perpetrator is often a child or students saying or doing things which highlight a variety of issues that they could be facing and dealing with. These could be students who have come from a poor emotional background with little if no positive role models and structure. They are often showing disrespect to the very person who can help them change and provide them with a better outlook and more positive view on life, yet their starting point is far from where they should be for this to be achieved. Therefore, here are a few things for you to consider should you be in the unfortunate position of having to deal with someone who hasn't managed as yet to know how good you are. Doing your utmost not to take it personally is always your starting point. Respect for others is you wanting to seek the best in them and for them – hold on to that thought whilst you seek to find out the cause of their disrespect.

Possible social and emotional causes

Age

Challenges to authority can occur from any age and can to be a response to avoid a consequence or a challenge to their view of how a situation should continue. From the age of 7 or 8 we tend to see the words 'that's not fair' creep into their conversation and interpretation of their experiences. Early adolescence is also the time for some to challenge those perceived to have control over their lives, and this continues through the teenage years. Society also has changed so that traditionally recognised positions of authority have become eroded. Blame is often looked for and along with blame goes a lowering of respect for the person they are seeking to blame.

Strategy

Shift from directing and commanding people to a more inclusive request as children develop in their lives. Remember you are teaching them communication as well as giving instructions. Tone of voice, as children get older, plays an important role in creating the right emotional reaction. Relying upon position or job title to gain respect needs to be replaced in the first place with good relationships. Respect tends to come from relationships rather than job title. First impressions and interactions lay a foundation on which to build and your calm respect towards them no matter what you encounter will make an impression.

A surprised reaction to their lack of respect and questioning in puzzlement as to why they have responded in such a fashion, linked with a reasonable request, opens dialogue. Social skills need for some to be explained, demonstrated, taught, and learnt. You might be the first person that their disrespect hasn't had a negative effect upon and therefore will register more in their mind.

Home/personal life

Parents and carers carry a lot of responsibility to teach social skills correctly. The once typical household and social environment for learning these has eroded and been replaced with little opportunity to learn and demonstrate social etiquette. Often, it has been replaced by various forms of media that promote more combative approach to authority and respect within their games and their social lessons are now learnt from whichever media device they watch or the people they mix with.

Strategy

Recognising your responsibility to demonstrate respect and correct forms of social etiquette is often key and these skills can indeed be taught as we as a species want to form cooperative relationships. Question the students one-to-one or in small groups to try to understand their perspective on authority and their choice of actions. Conversations about the environment at home need to be handled carefully and sometimes will require extra private time as you seek to find answers. Often the instructions that you are wishing them to follow are in marked contrast to those they have been given by their parents. I had one boy say to me that he has been instructed to punch people who have a go at him and never to worry about being in trouble as he (his dad) would always come and defend him. In a case like this, building a relationship is going to be key and will take time as you show politeness and interest in them. You will notice the respect towards you changing as you give them time and eventually you can start the process of them evaluating their own set of moral codes to live by. This has to be one that involves a positive outcome without the need for his dad to defend him. Be the difference they need – this is much better than responding to rudeness with punishment, which is never a recipe for mutual understanding

Relationship/belonging

People don't tend to be rude to people they feel a bond with. It is generally a good indicator of their thoughts regarding the situation they are finding themselves in or their attitude towards who you represent. School, by its very nature, has a lot of parts to it that alienate young people, Rudeness and disrespect highlight a lack of relationship and belonging. Another consequence of feeling rejected and lacking a sense of belonging with others is to show frustration and rudeness towards the very people or person they want to have a relationship with. Their actions are the very opposite of what will improve the situation but actually this sort of behaviour is very typical. It's like when a child comes and says to you, pointing at a group of other children, 'They are being horrible, and I hate them!' When you ask why, the explanation is often that it's because they won't let him play with them. When you go and speak with the other children, they point out that the child, when he was told he couldn't play with them, hit one of them.

Strategy

Forming relationships with those who initially are rude and disrespectful with no cause takes time as they have gone straight on the offensive. When dealing with someone at the age 12–14 peer pressure plays a strong role so any attempt at talking with them needs to be done away from others. Initially ask questions about them to find out as much as you can in as short a time as possible. Tell them something about what you do, if they don't already know. Only at the end of what they have shared ask them as to why they choose to be rude to you first without even knowing you. The very fact you are interested in them and listening to them is a good starting point. Remember, to change an attitude that is seated in disrespect will take time and the process will potentially have many setbacks. You may also have to accept that their rudeness will have resulted in a negative attitude from some members of staff who have experienced their onslaught in the past, and you may have to be sensitive to these colleagues' opinions as you work with them. If possible, pass on the good things that have happened so that other staff can see things are changing for the better. The more the person is made to feel included, even after the rudeness and disrespect, the more it will help in the process of them making better choices.

Self-esteem

Rudeness and lack of respect may well have causes outside of school and could link to many things which are affecting them personally. Often you may just be the consequence of how they are feeling about themselves and the situation they are in. Again, they may feel that attack is the best form of defence.

Strategy

As with many issues you experience, the starting point is for you to try to find out about their life and personal situation. Some of it may, because of child protection issues, have to remain private. The issues you are needing to know about should only be the ones in common knowledge, such as where they might be gaining social experiences outside of school and the folks who have an influence upon their lives now. What do they like to do in their free time? Who are their friends? And who do they most admire out of all the people they have known or heard about? These few questions can give you a quick insight into how their daily lives are and how they feel about themselves and those around them. You are seeking to know if they feel positive or negative about themselves as a possible reason as to why they go on the offensive. Get to know them. You might be the key that unlocks their confidence.

Possible challenges to sense of coherence

Model

Disrespect to those deemed to be in authority may, for some, have become the norm.

Strategy

Check with your colleagues to see whether this behaviour from the student is a commonly seen issue, whether it is a one off or the norm. Make sure you stay the same with them by demonstrating the correct way to speak and interact with others. Building a relationship will be key to changing the model. Consequences need to be given but in line with expectations and use that time to discover motive. If you find that others also have suffered the same lack of respect, then perhaps two or three of you can have a chat with him or her together as a group to ask of them what you all can do differently. Explain that you all, as teachers, want to do the best for the student, but at the moment there seems to be a struggle for you all to do so. If you are planning on trying this then be very explicit about why you are doing so as they will link it to the times when other adults have spoken to them as a group and it may not bring back good memories. So, explain you are doing so as you think the student, him or herself, can help all of you do a better job and improve the way you communicate and teach, so you are all after their help.

Having a few of you in a caring positive manner asking to understand and help them better will have an impression, especially if you all can collectively come up with a strategy that you are all willing to give a go to help turn things around. Which brings us neatly onto making it manageable for them.

Manageable

Some people have not been exposed in a positive way to new people who may influence their lives and they may not know how to start talking with someone new. Their contact in the past might have included people in authority, perhaps the police, social services. These professionals may have had an impact upon them or their family which has not been as positive as they would like, so they now treat all new people with the same negativity.

Also, if they have a reputation within school for being rude this will have built up over time and carried with it a lot of negative consequences. Unfortunately, this becomes learnt behaviour when approaching anyone new and is how they manage the situation. Without extra help, they will not have the skills to do anything different.

Strategy

Teach all your students the importance of first impressions and where possible introduce cover teachers to them and just spend a few minutes in one lesson talking about the expectations you have when they meet new people. Get feedback for when the class or some students have met an adult and it didn't go well. You could help teach someone how to manage their social interaction better. You can also ask them what they all thought about you when you first arrived and what feelings you generate when you start asking them to do things. Let them know that every interaction requires emotions and managing those emotions will go a long way to making the interactions positive. Time spent doing this for the whole class need only be five or ten minutes and can easily be linked into the outcomes of a lesson. New topics and new challenges are often like meeting new people, and you want them to learn the skills as soon as possible as you will be introducing new things to them continually. You are therefore helping them manage within lessons and topics as well as within the social arena.

Meaningful

As mentioned, respect has lost a lot of its social meaning in the lives of young people. In living for the now and in their own world, your interaction with them has no meaning and what you are expecting from them is not relevant either. The key to every interaction is that you have to become meaningful to them.

Strategy

Getting to know their own idea of respect and challenging them to live up to what they think is their own high standard is one conversation. Another would be to highlight to them that we need others to get on in life and the more skilled we can become in building relationships then the more successful we will become. You, having interactions within them around school as much as possible will lower the opportunity for disrespect. Try to make your first interaction with them wherever it may be as positive as you can. Be noticed when you are in school; walk around and visit other areas of the school. When in primary schools the younger children always ask me 'Who are you?', 'What are you doing here?', 'Are you going to teach us?', 'What's your name?' As they get older this verbal questioning disappears as they become silent ones asked in the mind. Get use to introducing yourself and notice how they respond. I am sad to say this will not always be as positive as you wish and may require follow up, but it's a start and I can guarantee it will reap rewards in the end. Make it meaningful for them to change – and that means making yourself meaningful to them.

Scenario 10: Students who find it hard to cope with the stress of everyday life

It is important to acknowledge the alarming rise in mental health issues in the young. The experiences you will encounter should provide you with greater understanding about what causes the stress and anxiety and various things that you, as a teacher, can do to help with children and students who mention to you about how they are feeling. The number of counsellors and support workers within school is on the increase. These support staff should be called upon if someone who comes to you feeling they are not able to cope with lessons or life needs more than a few words of encouragement and some strategies. Especially if you are finding you are needing to spend a lot of time with them and it affects your basic teaching responsibility for the others in your class. Most people would recognise when they feel healthy, relaxed and able to deal with all that life sends their way. But when issues start to mount up, they move from this relaxed state into recognising that they are now a bit less focused but still just about able to deal with things. At this point, when asked how they are, they would answer 'I am coping'. As things mount up even more, when asked how they are, they may say 'Now I am struggling', and if things don't change it is a small step to finding themselves unwell. This steady downward spiral is very typical for a lot of people.

I am very keen for you, as teachers, to recognise this pattern within the lives of those you teach, but more importantly to highlight there is a lot you can do when the students and young people are healthy, so you move them upwards to being securely mentally heathy or, as I like to call it, mentally secure. This builds upon their understanding that the more they develop the model, the more they can understand they have the ability to manage all they do, or at least that they have the resources available. By always working towards what is most meaningful for them, they will help maintain their own sense of coherence. Should this not be the case and they start to move to just coping, or struggling, here are a few things for you to consider and help address the decline.

Possible social and emotional causes

Age

Stress related issues are becoming more normal for young people as they face pressure often from adults to confirm or perform, with little emotional and social experience as to knowing what to do. The exposure to stress related issues such as friendships and the fear of rejection is often the biggest issue that young people face and starts from an early age. In the past, relationship issues often would have been solved by talking about things as they happen, but the rise in social media means that relationship breakdowns happen via text messaging, and often when miles apart, at different times of the day. Sometimes events happen late at night, meaning they are then unable to relax and sleep which makes sorting out the problems harder, leading to stress.

Strategy

When dealing with stress in young people, try to find the overall cause and relate your approach to developing their understanding of what is happening to them emotionally. We can all be emotional about situations but aim to help them develop emotional intelligence by looking at the various approaches to the emotion they are experiencing. Stress related problems are a part of everyday life and your aim is to help them develop their own strategies to cope and find solutions. Providing them with solutions means that you become the problem solver. With our life experiences as well as our understanding and maturity we can often see what needs to be done. But it's not necessarily the answers that are often needed. Seeking strategies that work for them is what you are after. This will only come by exploring what it is they want to achieve and what they have so far tried as well as what they think you can do about it. Sometimes the very time they spend talking to you briefly about it is enough for them to find clarity. I have listened to teachers and support staff solving so many issues by quick words of advice or stepping in to deal with a situation. While this may provide an immediate solution, it can leave the person ill equipped to manage when a similar issue arises. Question what they can do about it but remember that their age will influence their understanding. Getting them to see the bigger picture may make sense to a 16-year-old, but not to an 11-year-old.

Home/personal life

The very title covers a multitude of possibilities to add to the stress in life. Financial security or steady parent relationships are no guarantee that life will be stress free, as young people try to make sense of their world.

Strategy

When speaking to someone regarding stress, be ready to look at the possibilities that the root cause may indeed come from a variety of situations. It is the amount of them that is the overload. You may not be able to influence or change the situations they are having to face but your calmness and confidence that it can be managed will provide confidence for them as well as helping them to learn to cope better. Life is full of difficulties and we know that it would be wonderful if they would all go away yet it is through life's challenges that we learn resilience.

Relationship/belonging

By far the most common cause of stress or anxiety in young people is social rejection, or the fear of it. In the past this was often a way to learn how to become a good friend and develop those skills needed for emotional intelligence. Relationships conducted over social media often lead to misunderstanding and fallout, as has been previously mentioned. The generation you are teaching has grown up with social media and most interactions with friends are made through devices, which as we know can lead to a lot of misunderstandings. I believe over time the skill set for acceptability of contact will improve but in the mean time we still see issues spilling over into real life.

Strategy

Building a sense of belonging and discussing the importance of face-to-face relationships is key for helping them to develop social skills. Help them to understand the way the brain is developing and to look at the need to belong to others as a basic social skill. Help them seek to be the best person they can be by their standards first and foremost. Doing a quiz with your students and children regarding the positive way to communicate through social media will give you some insight into to what etiquette they all find acceptable. I was very disappointed to see my granddaughter return home with homework on bullying, its effects and what it is. Far better she returns home with homework about friends and how to become a good one, or on talking and being nice over social media. Extenuate the positive. Your relationship and letting them know you are there for them goes a long way to helping them learn to cope. When helping students to cope with a breakdown in relationships, ask them what three things they have tried already to fix it. Coach and mentor rather than trying to fix problems for them.

Self-esteem

Reflective questions relating to the situation they face are typical. This can often lead to students thinking that they are the one that has got it wrong, leading sometimes to them making the situation worse by trying too hard to be more liked by others.

Strategy

When trying to raise someone's self-esteem when it is related to relationship issues it's important to keep your praise realistic, grounded and focused on the future self, by talking about their characteristics and maturity. Help them to focus upon learning to like themselves rather than depending first and foremost on others liking them; that should come second. Also encourage them to seek out those with the same character as them and see if that helps.

Possible challenges to sense of coherence

Model

Orderliness and predictability tend to disappear when stress is happening, along with rational thinking and being able to see the bigger picture.

Strategy

In any stressful situation, find a routine that they can adopt that helps them see they are in control of something in their lives no matter what is going on externally. It could be as simple as taking a few moments to look at what is going on around them and doing nothing except observing people. It also might involve changing some aspect of what they normally do so as to redesign their usual day and look for a fresh perspective.

If they are interested in reading books there are many stories relating to various life challenges and how characters in the book overcame them. Speak to your librarian and see what they have and what may help for specific individuals.

Manageable

The main reason we become stressed is that our brain is searching for a solution to a problem that is important, and it is unable to find one. This often leads to us doing the same thing over and over again, hoping that the problem will be sorted the next time we do it.

Strategy

In life often we cannot manage the situation we face as the situation is beyond our control. Help them to focus upon what they can manage, and then to do something about that. If you can't change the situation then change the attitude towards the situation. If constant worry is a theme then ask them to only worry for 15 minutes, i.e. from 5.15 to 5.30 and when they do start to worry if it is outside of that period then to wait until it is that time. Helping others is often a very good way to stop dwelling on oneself. See if you can ask them to become a helper of yours either within the classroom or for another teacher who has a new student arriving perhaps and would benefit from having someone show them around and talk to them. There are also small clubs within most schools always on the lookout for help during lunch or break time. Knowing what your school does and what is needed is always good for you to know and to be able to tap into if needed.

Meaningful

The reason that we have become stressed is because the situation is impacting upon something that we find meaningful.

Strategy

Not all stress is harmful as it is causing us to become focused and look for strategies to change an unwelcome situation. Help students to find the most meaningful thing in their life and then see how you can relate the solving or managing of the situation to that one thing. Look also to see how they have managed a stressful situation in the past and let them understand that the more they learn to manage and cope the calmer their mind will become during stressful situations. As mentioned, all these strategies can and should be thought about whilst the children and students are well. This will go a long way to helping them find coping strategies for when things go a little pear shaped. Any conversation that a student may have with you also has the danger of becoming one that they have had with others as well so check that you are not just one of many this issue is being discussed with, as this in itself for some students becomes part of their meaningful though unhelpful strategy. Talking about it might help yet we are looking for solutions.

Scenario 11: Interrupting, shouting out

Possible social and emotional causes

Age

Throughout both primary and secondary age groups you will come across children and students who constantly want to interrupt the lesson by either asking questions or by answering questions by shouting out when you have specifically asked for them to put their hands up before answering. This has more to do with their inability to rein in a natural tendency to speak and to be included in the world around them rather than them being rude and not thinking. You will see them, out of lessons, interrupting their friends and constantly talking, and possibly this will be a situation being dealt with in other classes. The school and the classroom system are hard places for them to learn to rein in their enthusiasm and natural tendencies and for some this is a long way off without some form of help and strategies. It is the opposite of those children and young people who are always quiet in class and reticent to put their hands up and answer questions.

Strategies

There are a variety of ways you can help them start the process of self-regulation but it will need outside assistance, as to rely upon the strategies alone will meet with frustration for the students as well as yourself.

1. Standing near them and preparing them for the questions
    Before you embark on asking the class questions and looking for answers, remind the class as a whole what is expected and help them to engage some self-management before the questions start. Standing near to the child will also help. Give them a thumbs up every time they resist the urge to shout out. They may be making other noises to get your attention, and this can be addressed later. Congratulate them and add, 'I'm very impressed with how you managed yourself.' Help them see that you recognise them trying.
2. Lollipop sticks
    At the start of the lesson, hand them five lollipop sticks and say that every time they make a comment or ask a question they must first hand over a lollipop stick. It will help them to start to regulate the amount of times they shout out, as well as helping them to reflect on the value of their answer or comment.
3. Enlist friends
    Speak with them and their friends. Highlight the fact that you are going to try to help the child not shout out and you need their help as well to help him stay quiet. Then ask them what they think they could do, and what does the child concerned think their friends could do? Pass the issue to them and see how they start to solve it.

Home/personal life

Some home lives are extremely noisy and often chaotic, with children vying for attention with the parents or carers. The need to be included and listened to, by being loud and interrupting, often overspills into the classroom.

Strategies

If possible, speak with the parents or the child regarding the situation at home and see if it is similar to how they conduct themselves at school. Help the child to realise that within the classroom, as time is very limited and everyone should have an opportunity to speak and be heard, you, as the teacher, need them to get used to taking turns to speak and you will make sure they will have theirs. Explain you are interested in their answers as well as their comments and encourage them to find appropriate ways of explaining things to you by the work they produce.

Relationship/belonging

Being heard is an important aspect of feeling valued. If you have a good relationship with the young person or students, then that in itself may be a cause of them wanting to show off to you and demonstrate how knowledgeable they are of your subject. It may also highlight that they don't have a very good relationship with the rest of the class, and you are their one and only focal point.

Strategies

If you think this may be an issue, ask them what they think you like students to do when you ask questions. See if they know what they are meant to do. If they answer correctly, ask them why they think you like it when the class puts their hands up and doesn't shout out? Then you can ask them why they do things differently and not as you would like, since they know what to do. Then ask them what they think you can do to help them get it right.

Encourage them to work with you next time you ask questions or are speaking to the class, as you would really like them to try to do the right thing next time.

If they don't seem to have bonded in any meaningful way with anyone in the class, they may be wanting your attention. If you think this is the case, then link them with another person for a specific role and/or duty so they start to cooperate and work with others. For example, you could give them a role collecting or distributing books, or being a table monitor, or coaching others within the class who need some extra help. At the end of the lesson commend them both for how well they have worked together if they have done so.

Self-esteem

One possible issue of shouting out especially if doing so attracts the attention of others in the class could hide the fact they don't have friends who wish to mix with them outside of lessons. Often the class comic can become a lonely person. This in turn leads them to constantly hear from others that their behaviour is poor or silly or immature building up a picture which says more about their actions than it does about them as a person. It also can become a solution in itself as whilst you are dealing with the shouting out, they are receiving attention from you as well as other children and students.

Strategies

The content of the shouting out will give you some indication as to the motive. If it is tending to try to be funny, rude or informative regarding the lesson content, each one of these will indicate the intended audience. Speak to them regarding your conclusion of their motive to ascertain if it is correct and then you can look at possible alternative strategies for them to achieve their desire. Highlight at all times their value to you as a member of the class and look to find a way for them to contribute in an orderly fashion so as not to diminish from the content if it has merit.

Possible challenges to sense of coherence

Model

Any changes have the potential to raise anxiety in some students, which can often lead to them becoming over excited. Starting a new topic, introducing new learning, moving people around in the room or class will cause those who are talkative to talk more as it is a way to manage the new situation.

Strategies

Consistency in all you do is key, and if you have to use prompts to help them control themselves then the more often you use them the quicker they will get used to complying. As you meet them at the door you can remind them of what you are going to do to help them control themselves better. Reminding before it happens is far better and will provide more opportunity for success.

Manageable

To change what is for some a habit that has become part of who they are and how they communicate will take time. Those students I have asked all say to me that they try to stop shouting out, but they keep getting it wrong.

What you are asking them to do requires them to be able to change the way that they have lived their life at home and throughout their experience within school. You will probably not be the first to have encouraged them to change, and because it is still an issue they begin to think that they just can't manage it. It is part of who they are. The ability to re-wire the brain to stop this will need help. Positive re-enforcement will work well.

Strategies

Discuss with them if they would like to work with you to help them stop shouting out, so they don't get into trouble. Tell them that you are going to work with them and help them. Let them know it will be a combined effort and 'we' will succeed.

Meaningful

The amount of times they will have heard their name called out by the teacher and told to stop doing something will generally be enough encouragement for them to want that situation to change.

Strategy

Ask them the questions, 'What would it be like if you have a day when you don't get told off?', 'Who would you tell first?', 'How happy and impressed would they be with you?' This is usually enough of a motivating factor for them to work with you to help them to re-wire their brain and to start to control their natural tendencies.

But just as if I ask you to only use your non-regular hand to turn on the lights at home, whilst I am with you and reminding you, you will succeed, but it will take a while before it becomes the norm. *On average, it takes more than two months before a new behaviour becomes automatic – 66 days to be exact.* And how long it takes a new habit to form can vary widely depending on the behaviour, the person, and the circumstances. Phillippa Lally, a health psychology researcher at University College London, conducted a research project which found that it took anywhere from 18 days to 254 days for people to form a new habit (Lally et al., 2009).

Remember: your patience will help, it takes time and encouragement.

Scenario 12: Friendship/relationship problems

The classroom works well when everyone cooperates and shows levels of respect towards each other; and the opposite is true when you have relationship problems arising which prevent effective learning as well as creating a negative atmosphere within the class. This often leads, if unresolved quickly, to parents being involved and eventually, if no successful outcome is found, to students or children changing class. This, in itself, is disruptive to the students as well as the new class which they have been moved to. It is therefore important as soon as possible to work towards building a team ethos in your class, where people can get to know each other, appreciate their differences and learn to be able to work with others. Falling out amongst children does and will occur as individuals find their own identity and friendship groups. Part of distinguishing themselves as a group is to highlight how someone who isn't part of their group is different. It is part of growing up. How you manage it will help them not only through school but through life as they meet new people and have to work and get along with them. Not many friendships last from school days as it's a forced environment where people are put together for admin and age reasons. Only later, in university, college or work, when people have choices and the experience of making and keeping friends has been learnt, will lasting lifelong friendships start to be made.

Whilst in your class as they learn this social skill, the children and students will need help in managing some of the emotions that can arise.

Often friends are separated for fear of them distracting each other and not doing the work. I tend to keep friends together so they can learn support and encouragement and self-control. They will then learn and develop from a friendship of mutual fun and pleasure of each other's company into a friendship of respect and support. It will often take more time as you explain what it is you are looking for from them and coach them into recognising the benefits of being supportive friends with each other, but you will be well rewarded by the work they produce. However, if issues should arise here are a few things to consider.

Possible social and emotional causes

Age

Friendships, making them, keeping them and becoming a good friend is a social skill learnt during our younger years and, like all things, we tend to learn through experience. Those experiences are not always nice but can be beneficial. You don't have to teach friendship, as children will naturally recognise what is a good friendship by the way they feel they are being treated. They also learn the rules of friendship through play – coming to understand that it is reciprocal, mutual, reliable and rewarding. Though you may not need to teach them the rules they will need a supportive and steady environment for this social skill to develop. At ages 4 to 7, reciprocal play is key to a good friendship as they learn to take on roles and give one another directions. At age 7, talking to each other becomes important as they discuss more independent things and look to keep secrets from adults, bonding together in a shared motivation of getting along in the situations in which they find themselves. At 12 years of age, as they enter secondary school, they begin to share confidences – which is why betrayal of those confidences can feel overwhelming. Group identity reaches its climax at around the age of 14. You will see who is in and who is out, and a social ladder forms where the most popular children make up 15% of the class; the accepted group, 45%; the average group, 20%; and the unclassified, 20%.

Strategies

Do your utmost to let them try to sort out their issues themselves. Ask them to think about what they cando themselves. What would they like to do? What about finding a different person to be friends with? Most of the upsets they have at an early age they will learn from and the upset will soon be forgotten.

Make opportunities to mix people within the classroom to widen the social network. Help them to understand that they are just as accountable for their behaviour to each other during these times. Highlight the skills needed to work and succeed together and use the point about accountability of actions should things go wrong. For the more isolated children see if the school can arrange friendship groups where they can meet and connect with each other. Six to eight of such meetings can have a positive impact.

Home/personal life

Eighty percent of the children in your class, even though they might fall out with friends at times, will tend to have at least one good friend who will stick with them and be there for them and with them. The bottom 20% is of more concern as they fall into three categories: neglected children (5%), who tend to be shy, very close to their families and good students; controversial children (5%), who tend to have traits that some of their peers like but they also have annoying habits; rejected children (10%), are overly aggressive from the start and tend to be more aggressive if rejected by others, leading them to become more withdrawn. This will also be the situation outside of your classroom and manifest itself within their homelife as well.

Strategies

Your classroom needs to be a socially all-inclusive environment, and you must make this clear right from the start. Social etiquette can be discussed and an agreed way of working and accepting each other to work towards the common aim will help lay a platform on which to build. For those who you recognise as being more at risk, arrange seating plans that encourage cooperative working, with them included. Coach the controversial children to help them give up on annoying habits. For those who show more persistent aggression, the policy of 'keeping hands and feet to yourselves', which tends to be introduced at an early age in schools, should be reinforced. Aggression may link to a variety of other issues that will be for the pastoral team to investigate. Talk with parents and see if their child is able to mix with others outside of school in any group activity where they have the opportunity to learn to mix more with others.

Possible challenges to sense of coherence

Model

Relationships can become strained if something has happened outside of the normal expected routine of the friendship. Seating plans are often a cause of resentment amongst KS2/3 children, as they want to be more in charge of where they sit and who they interreact with – being forced to sit with someone outside of their own group may cause issues. Unexpected changes in the way people act towards each other also cause issues.

Strategies

Be aware that any changes that you might make, however small, can affect the relationship connection between those within your classroom. You must manage any changes in a sensitive manner, initially by highlighting the responsibility of actions and reactions. Explain why you are making the changes and make them meaningful for the students as well as you. Thank them when they do make the changes you suggest.

If fallings out occur because of the way the students have acted towards each other, remember that learning about friends and others is their learning experience so ask them when you have some time with them to repair the damage you witnessed in the classroom. Start by highlighting that you are not necessarily interested in what led up to the event but more in what they have learnt about the situation, and then challenge them to look at their own reactions and behaviour in light of the situation. How did what they do improve or resolve the issue? Explain relationships need work and either a relationship is worth working at because of the mutual benefit to each other or it is not, and they can decide what to do about it. If they decide to not continue with their friendship then encourage them to talk about what it was they did like about each other when they first met. Relationships can end just by moving on.

Manageable

Friendship and relationship require work and, as we know, people are often hard work. It is not surprising that you will encounter students and young people at a loss to know what to do and how to react during tricky times. This will inevitably lead them to head to an adult to solve the issue for them.

Strategies

Listen to them and appreciate how important it is and the emotion they are feeling about the situation. Remind them of what you are expecting them to be doing and focusing on within your lesson and, if possible, address the issue with them away from the rest of the class at a time convenient to you both. They may be showing anger and frustration about the situation and your listening calmly to them will help them also calm down. Asking them to focus upon the task you have set will help. When you get time, you should aim to be a listener and enquirer as to what they are intending to do about things, then steer them towards understanding of the consequences of what they may wish to do. It is important that they themselves learn through these events; they will instinctively know what they should do, and the ways they can solve the situation. Encourage them to stay away from social media and posting anything negative about the situation.

Meaningful

Not feeling part of the group and not feeling accepted, whether in the classroom or outside of the classroom, is the biggest cause of anxiety with young people. For some, nothing is more important than having that sense of belonging with a group of people that they wish to be friends with. It is important that you recognise the significance of isolation and the negative impact this can have.

Strategies

Within your classroom, look for the social breakdown of relationships and manage as much as possible the inclusion of everyone to widen the feeling of acceptance, empathy and understanding across the classroom. Make inclusion key to your introduction of things that you will be looking for, and deal with any incidents by talking with them about their behaviour to one another as soon as things occur. This need only take a couple of minutes at the end of the lesson, to remind them of their social responsibility to others as well as their own accountability for their actions.

Scenario 13: Low self-esteem

Self-esteem has been shown to have an effect upon our cognition, motivation, emotions and behaviour, which is why it's important for us to recognise the importance of developing self-esteem within the students we teach. We, as teachers, need to be able to recognise those with a negative outlook upon themselves and upon what they believe they are able to achieve and be sure that we are providing them with opportunities to succeed and celebrate their successes.

I have worked in schools that use the adage, 'Even better if …' to encourage students to look at what they have achieved and ask the question of how it could have been even better if. The merits of the question I can understand if it comes after a proper celebration of an achievement and the person has a motivation for improvement at the time of asking. For some it can highlight that yet again they could have done better, thus reinforcing a detrimental effect upon their view of themselves as well as having an adverse effect on their relationship with the teacher as the person who is not satisfied with what they achieve. Your comments and your words of recognition can go a long way to building up a student's low self-esteem.

Possible social and emotional causes

Age

The starting point of the problem can be from a young age as the child is exploring their own ability to learn and trying new things. The response from those around them, watching and being with them as they explore, will be helping them to create a view of themselves. The influence of parents, carers and other peers, as well as significant adults such as teachers and other members of the support team, all play a part in the child's perception. Their own physical appearance and how accepted they feel when they meet people, and comments that have been made, will also impact on their self-esteem. There are no throwaway lines or comments when it comes to the effects of our words on the lives of young people. If you have someone with low self-esteem in your class, here are some things to consider.

Strategies

With any young person when trying to build them up make your praise comments measured and specific. They are very competent in recognising false over the top praise. Assign specific achievable tasks for them within the classroom. Spend the same amount of time with them as with others and include them in positive comments if appropriate with the rest of the class. You will need to be sensitive about doing so and it will be best if you include their name along with others when doing so, linking them with other successful and established people within the class.

Home/personal life

Home life can have a strong influence on perceptions, and it would be lovely to think that all households are supportive and encouraging. Sometimes the methods used to encourage can unfortunately have a detrimental effect upon the wellbeing of an individual – for example, constantly being told things like: 'You shouldn't do that', 'Why don't you think!', 'Stop being a pain'. I am sure you can add to the list of comments that are made to young children. Your influence and responsibility are for your classroom and the environment that you create around it and sometimes even innocent comments might trigger a reminder of what they have been told or heard at home or elsewhere.

Strategies

During parents' evenings, should you or your colleagues have a chance to talk with the parents or carers of the child you have concerns about, encourage them all to talk about any positive aspects of their child, highlighting positive things they have noticed and like. Steer them towards how positive remarks will breed positive responses and ask what they can do at home to build upon what you are doing at school. See if you can open a positive dialogue with the parents to continue informing each other of good things over the next term.

Relationship/belonging

As young people grow and mature, they continually assess and compare themselves with those they either see around them or they see within social media. Those with low self-esteem tend to be hypersensitive, not only to the fact that in their view they don't measure up to the expected standards of others but also to the comments and actions from others and can be easily hurt.

They also tend to be 'hypervigilant and hyperalert to signs of rejection, inadequacy, and rebuff' (Rosenberg and Owens, 2001). Often, individuals lacking self-esteem see rejection and disapproval even when there isn't any. 'The danger always lurks that [they] will make a mistake, use poor judgement, do something embarrassing, expose [themselves] to ridicule, behave immorally or contemptibly. Life, in all its variety, poses on ongoing threat to the self-esteem.'

With all this in mind you can see that your classroom is a place where you need to be very aware as to the comments not only from you but also from others which can add to the stress and negativity which others might be feeling. Those who are just starting to feel less about themselves because of a variety of issues – physical, emotional, social – need to be able to feel safe and have the sense of belonging within your classroom.

Strategies

It has often been said that the best things in life are not things, and this outlook should be encouraged within the classroom. Self-esteem can be addressed by the person having a more honest approach and overview of themselves. This can be done with the help of a pastoral worker within your school if it is seen as necessary. In the meantime, within your classroom highlight with everyone the importance of their personal values and principles and help them to evaluate what they do and achieve. Praise them for how they have tackled things, their resolve, commitment, resilience and patience. The list of important meaningful things is very large, and these should be the foundation of all your praise and recognition. Talk with anyone who you feel has a low opinion of their work and/or ability and ask them about their own values. Highlight to them characteristics that you have noticed that you like and encourage them to be the best person they can be with all they have. The measure is the one they set themselves based upon themselves. Also, a way to help raise self-esteem is to give the person an opportunity to help others and to feel useful, so look for opportunities that encourage mutual support and cooperation. This will have the added advantage of improving a sense of belonging within the group they work with.

Possible challenges to sense of coherence

Model

The view a person can have of themselves may be false and harmful to their self-esteem, yet it can in some instances become the normal expression that they use when talking about themselves to others: 'I am useless at that', 'No one likes me', 'I hate the way I look'. The list can go on, covering a variety of issues and become part of the normal everyday comments made by a person about themselves. Some students may be saying these things in order to hear the person they are saying it to counteract their comment with a positive one. Whatever the reason, if it has become a habit and it has become the model that is familiar and therefore embedded to them. As they hear those words, however false, they invest in them a meaning of truth which affects their true appreciation of their worth and value.

Strategies

The question 'why?' is often underused by people when trying to understand the motives of others. We are usually very good at interpreting why people do what they do, yet when asked have they actually asked the person themselves the answer is often no. So, if you have someone who makes negative comments about themselves, do some investigating with them and ask them if they have noticed that they do it? Ask them the question, 'Why do you do so, especially when those around you think the opposite?' Do so in an interview-type way, being curious, and look also to explore the possibility that they may, in a way, be preventing themselves being different or better than they think, as they have given themselves a verdict that can't change. The aim is to see if you can encourage a change in the model in their head as well as a model in their conversation so that a new more honest view of themselves can start to be used. Look for alternative comments and encourage them to repeat to you positive words they have heard others saying about themselves.

Manageable

Life coaches, self-help books, inspirational quotes and thoughts for the day, are extremely popular and are used by people in a variety of ways to help them form a positive view of themselves and their view of the world, as well as how they can tackle situations within their lives. To talk to someone who has low self-esteem it naturally follows that they will have low confidence in their own ability to change their view of themselves, therefore they will need to know they can change their perception with the help of trusted others. You, as a teacher, who is there to improve the life chances and wisdom of the individuals you teach should also be the one to help raise their consciousness of themselves to a realistic level.

Strategies

In all your dealings with all your staff build a reputation of honest feedback and appraisal. Make sure your words that encourage and commend, are ones of balance. The aim is for your words to have value when you say things and if possible, have them carry an explanation as to why you are giving the praise. For those with low self-esteem ask them to repeat the words that you say back to you with the explanation, and with a smile.

'What did I just say?'
'Why did I like it?'
'What was good about it?'
'What do you think about what I have said?'

For the last question, if they disagree with you, you may need to help them search through the answers of the previous questions to find the flaw in their opinion. Remember that self-esteem is more about the person and this is the area in which your help will be most needed. After talking about the work, you can speak about how you enjoy teaching them, how pleased you are that they are in your class, how impressed you are with ... whatever you have found from them that impresses you. Feeling valued by others is often a good starting point to feeling valued by yourself.

Meaningful

It is often very hard for someone with low self-esteem to find things meaningful for themselves.

Strategies

Within the classroom you can seek their assistance to help you and speak to them regarding how you really would appreciate if they could do ... for you. Build up a relationship to also build their confidence whilst they are with you. See if your colleagues could do similar things so that you can share positive comments about the student back to them when you see them next. Also, if your school has lunch time quiet places for some students, see if they could go along and support the students there. Be specific that you are wanting them to help and express your belief that they will be good at it. Look also to see if the person can assist in helping younger students, with reading or simple maths or just being a buddy as they settle in. Help them focus upon others to find their usefulness for themselves and provide them with a task that becomes both meaningful and rewarding.

Scenario 14: Silly disruptive behaviour in class

Throughout your teaching you will inevitably witness a variety of disruptive behaviour within your classroom. Some if it will be funny, other situations will be distressing, yet all of it will have a reason and your role will be one of looking for the reason first and then through this understanding dealing with the disruption.

A situation which can become very draining on the patience of adults in the room is when a child decides they want to be funny or amusing, or simply wants to engage in behaviour that to them is amusing.

It helps if you remember that fun in the classroom and having a laugh and smiling is a good thing and will go a long way to making your lessons memorable as well as enjoyable. Being funny, though, is a skill and often the behaviour of children and young people falls short of the mark as it often has a victim or is quite simply disruptive. Their behaviour is rewarding on some level to them though, and if you can discern who the intended audience is for their antics, that will give you an idea of what it is they are trying to achieve and help you to redirect the same reward through a far more constructive set of behaviours.

We often listen to celebrity comedians on the TV. Sir Lenny Henry, for example, who acknowledges he was the class clown, recognises he learnt some of his early techniques by mimicking the teachers in his school. Unfortunately, not all class clowns are so gifted, destined for a knighthood and global recognition; instead, they simply remain a disruptive and annoying influence on the environment in which you are aiming to teach. Their behaviour can range from making sarcastic comments or acting out different situations (from a football fan to a monkey), to barking like a dog, or making other noises constantly. They may repeat the words others have said and annoy the person they are repeating; they may take others' pens or books and run around the room with them. Younger ones may crawl under desks or simply run around the classroom. As you can see, it may take various forms and be highly amusing for the person performing the action or behaviour, yet can be equally as annoying for others, especially if you are trying to keep the rest of the class on task and focused. All of the above in various degrees will capture the attention of others. You will also recognise that these behaviours are going to be associated more with younger children. The older students witnessing such behaviour (14–15+) will, in contrast, be able to recognise it is immature and that it is taking away from their own learning. The pressures exerted by their peers to stop is often a mechanism for the misbehavers to curb their immature antics. You will still have 'childish' behaviour from this older age group but nothing as varied. It might be a time to see if some of their 'skills' and need for an audience could be encouraged to have a more constructive outcome by performing on the school stage. But before this burst into possible fame, you may experience far more childish behaviour impacting upon your class, so what is it you need to take into account and what can you do about it?

Age

As mentioned, a lot of the childish behaviour is associated with, as the name suggests, childishness. The simple act of being a child and doing what children naturally do is understandable and thankfully appropriate, yet as the conformity of the classroom starts to impact upon the normal free flow of activity associated with Year 1 then the acting out of the childish behaviour overflows into the classroom. The strength of mental ability needed to curb natural behaviour and to conform will be dependent upon a lot of extenuating circumstances. Telling a 5–7-year-old to control themselves and stop doing things which you think are inappropriate will be met with a variety of outcomes, and very seldom will it be successful. This is an emotional intelligence skill and the lack of it at a young age can start to signal to you as an adult that the child might have other underlying problems, not just a lack of emotional ability.

Strategies

With the younger ones, if possible, talk with their parents to see if they can work with you to on a reward plan for the child, looking at the times they are able to curb their disruptive behaviour. Focus on success and length of concentration time and look at increasing it. We have discussed the amount of time young children can concentrate and this may need to be adjusted for specific individuals. Also, the younger ones may need more one-to-one intervention and help within the classroom to encourage positive behaviour and cooperation. Look for trigger times of the day or trigger events which may be a reason for their silliness. For those over the age of 8 I would recommend one-to-one conversations focusing upon their understanding of their behaviour and how it is affecting your role as an teacher. Do so in a fact-finding way and let them know you are not looking to tell them off, just to engage with them so they can appreciate the long-term impact of what they are doing for themselves as well as their classmates. You could also, at this stage, ask them to enlist the help of a friend to help curb their enthusiasm for silly behaviour and set a reward system for both of them should you all see an improvement by the end of the week. It could involve you calling home to commend both children for their positive cooperation.

Home/personal life

Quite a lot of the behaviour you witness within the classroom will have its origins in the home and the kind of environment the young person has experienced or been associated with. Quite a number of poor behaviours, some even at the opposite end of the scale from being a class clown, like being very timid and withdrawn, can be a sign that things at home may be having an effect upon how they perceive the world as well as their role within it. A number of children are found to be very amusing by adults when they do silly outlandish things and getting an approving comment from adults may in fact be the encouragement needed to carry on with such behaviour at school. We all tend to work towards attention seeking in one form or another. Young children may have learned inappropriate behaviour as a way of attention seeking, and a mechanism for getting at least some form of recognition.

Strategies

Check with parents about the kind of behaviour seen at home, and also check for what is and isn't acceptable behaviour at home. Ask how the parents or carers interact with them as this could give you some idea about how much of the unwanted behaviours they see as well as how appropriate it might be. I remember my wife asking a mother of a child how much do they read or play with their child and the response she got was said with some surprise at the idea. 'I no read to him, I no play with him. He have phone he on phone when he home.' The answer enabled the school to put into place some strategies to help the child to appreciate and play nicely with others, because when the child was in the classroom surrounded by so many peers, his behaviour was 'silly' and disruptive as he just wanted to mix with them and interact with them. This brings us on to the next section to think about.

Relationships and belonging

As a social species, we long for and seek interaction, approval and acceptance from others. In years gone past, quite often the social normalities of what is and isn't acceptable were learnt through times of unstructured play. As this is for some now a thing of the past, when children do come together their interactions are usually full of the normal problems associated with people learning to get along with each other. The idea that silly behaviour is designed to either make oneself noticeable and, in some way, acceptable to others has long been understood. Some children unfortunately practise this in your classroom. It can demonstrate their need for acceptance and recognition.

Strategies

Look to see if the silly behaviours are acceptable with others in the class and look for the intended audience. Sometimes boys do silly things to attract the attention of girls – they may have learned that being silly with their other boy mates wins them approval, yet when they try the same techniques with girls they get a different response. Unfortunately, this tends to encourage the boys to try the techniques even more. Speak with them about the reasons they do what they do. If they respond, 'I don't know, I just do it', ask them would they like to try doing something else instead, which keeps them occupied but is also helpful to you and their classmates as well. Then think of a role you can ask them to do which helps work towards them needing to act more maturely. This can work for any age from 5 onwards.

Possible challenges to sense of coherence

Model

Any changes cause a variety of actions, as we now understand, so when confronted with a child or student being silly and disruptive ask about their lives in general and what they have been up to. Is there anything going on at home that might have changed? A new baby in the house, perhaps? Or are they moving to a new house?

Strategies

If something has changed, giving them a chance to talk about it will in some ways help settle them. You may not have time to go into too much detail within the classroom so enlist the help of support staff to find out more and then relay what has been discovered back to you. In the meantime, your concern and attention may alleviate the need to be silly.

Manageable

The pressure of learning within the classroom along with all the other social and emotional aspects of life in general can become very tiring. It doesn't take too much energy to be disruptive though. The energy gained off those who are on the receiving end of the disruption can in fact keep fuelling the poor behaviour. Managing oneself can also be tiring and requires a lot of mental ability. Young children and students often drink and eat items packed with sugar, which makes the task of self-regulation even tougher.

Strategies

Enlist the help of the whole class to aim to be as calm as possible during any disruptive event. Let everyone know, in order to minimalise any disruption, then as a class you can seek to establish a recognised plan. You can introduce this at any point, and preferably before any disruption or silly behaviour has started to occur. For the younger ones, you normally will get a small window of opportunity within the first week or so, when you can highlight what you require from them in specific situations. You can even link it to what they should all do if a fire alarm goes off. You require them all to be calm and sensible as the starting point. You can then have a discussion about what you should all do if someone does … and then give them some situations. The less people react, the harder the person has to work at being disruptive. We know food and drink will also have an impact so check what they have eaten and drunk that also might make it hard for them to rein in their behaviour. For the older students, you can even have a chat with them and their friends to seek a more mature approach to lessons and ask them what they find hard in their managing of their behaviour and what you could do to help them. Phoning home for some becomes embarrassing as they get older, even if this may have had a good effect when they were young, so use this as a pretext for them starting to take charge.

Meaningful

The behaviour will have meaning and purpose, so finding out what that is will enable you to better direct their approach towards achieving their own aims.

Strategies

The more you ask questions, seeking to understand what it is the child or student wants to avoid or achieve, the better it will be for you to help them work towards a more positive outcome for all. With young children, it might just be that they want some attention, and don't mind how they get it, so you may have to provide them with support outside of lessons for them to work through this need. If doing so it is vital that the links with the class and students within are maintained as much as possible. Try to make sure that any interventions take place during break time with their friends, so they can talk through as well as work through their need. With older children it might highlight a lack of appreciation as to why they are doing the lesson in the first place and therefore to disrupt, be silly and annoying is simply a method of them highlighting their frustration. Again, your chats with them should focus upon what is meaningful and then highlight ways of learning to manage with frustrating things in a more mature fashion.

Whatever the reason for silly disruptive behaviour, it can become very annoying, very quickly, as it highlights the exact opposite of what you are aiming to achieve within your classroom. Please remember it is an expression of communication, and just like everything else you have to contend with, your example of calmness and emotional intelligence will help them find a better way of communicating with you.

References

Lally, P., van Jaarsfeld, C. H. M., Potts, H. M. M. and Wardle, J. (2009). 'How habits are formed: modelling habit formation in the real world', *European Journal of Social Psychology*, 40(6), 998–1009.

Rosenberg, M. and Owens, T. J. (2001). 'Low self-esteem people: a collective portrait'. In T. J. Owens, S. Stryker, and N. Goodman (eds) *Extending Self-esteem Theory and Research: Sociological and Psychological Concerns*. Cambridge: Cambridge University Press.

And finally

There are a great many resources out there to help you in your teaching career. I am often asked to recommend either books or people to go and listen to. Like most things in life, many of these recommendations are made from personal choices and preferences. The books I like to recommend focus on our understanding of emotional intelligence. I always recommend people learn as much as they can about emotional intelligence as most of their days are going to be spent either dealing with it or the lack of it with people, and the more you know and understand, the more patience you can bring to situations. I do like to recommend the book, *The Boy Who Was Raised as a Dog* by Bruce Perry and Maia Szalavitz (published in 2006 by Basic Books, Philadelphia). This book was recommended to me by my daughter whilst studying for her psychology degree. Dr Perry explains the effects on the emotional and social brains of young people who have experienced trauma. The book holds no punches regarding the sad lives some children have gone through, but it also highlights the impact of kind words and care by the people these young children meet later in life.

I also recommend to teachers – especially those who wish to know all that is going on within the world of education – to join Tony Stephens' subscription website. He publishes a fortnightly newsletter, 'Academy and School News Updates'. He manages to bring together details about all new important documentation that has been issued, including all government publications, educational reports and research policies. His website also contains over 2000 key educational documents that have been published over recent years. If you are new to the profession it helps bring you up-to-date with everything affecting the industry and, as you progress in your leadership, it will provide you with the necessary resources to help you develop your work within the school with a wide range of school improvement documents.

He can be contacted at tonystephens856@gmail.com – just let him know Victor sent you.

Index

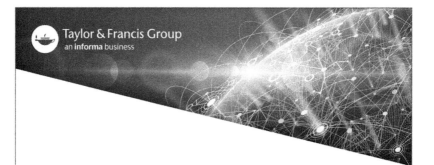

.

www.ingramcontent.com/pod-product-compliance
Ingram Content Group UK Ltd.
Pitfield, Milton Keynes, MK11 3LW, UK
UKHW010020280225
455677UK00023B/717